A THEOLOGY OF THE OLD TESTAMENT

A Theology of the Old Testament

Timothy P. Palmer

AFRICA CHRISTIAN TEXTBOOKS

2014

A Theology of the Old Testament

© 2011 Timothy P. Palmer

Africa Christian Textbooks (ACTS)

ACTS Bookshop, International HQ, TCNN,
PMB 2020, Bukuru, Plateau State, 930008, Nigeria
GSM: +234 (0) 803-589-5328; E-mail: pa@actsnigeria.org
Website: http://actsnigeria.org

ISBN: 9789789051175 Print
ISBN: 9789789053421 ePub
ISBN: 9789789053438 Mobi

CONTENTS

PREFACE

The Old Testament is a favorite part of the Bible for the African Christian. The culture of the Old Testament is similar to the traditional African culture. The Old Testament also has a large number of stories which appeal to the African.

But a problem with the Old Testament is that it is old.[1] The Old Testament is in a sense pre-Christian even though it proclaims Jesus Christ. In addition, the Old Testament is large and complex.

This Old Testament theology attempts to identify some main themes in the Old Testament. Of course this is not easy since there is such diversity in this part of Scripture. Yet we believe that there is an essential harmony in Scripture that allows us to trace some of these main themes. This is partly true because of the divine inspiration of all of Scripture.

This book has evangelical presuppositions. We believe that all of Scripture is God-breathed and authoritative for life and doctrine (2 Tim 3:16). We believe that there is both a human and divine author of all of Scripture.

This book was developed as a result of my teaching at the Theological College of Northern Nigeria in Bukuru. I wish to express my gratitude especially to the students of TCNN who have always been lively participants in the exercise of Old Testament theology. I also express my gratitude to the proprietors of TCNN who have given me the privilege ofteaching in this fine institution for more than 25 years.

I want to thank those who have taken time to read this manuscript and have given useful input into this book. *Na gode!* Thank you!

---

[1]C. Wright, *Living as the People of God*, p. 12.

It is my prayer that this book will be used for the edification of Christ's church and kingdom in Africa and beyond.

Christmas 2010
Theological College of Northern Nigeria
Bukuru

CHAPTER 1

THE LIVING GOD

The Old Testament is about God. Like the African, every Israelite believed in God. It is Yahweh God who created us and who leads us.

Only the fool will say, "There is no God" (Ps 14:1), and this fool does not really deny the existence of God but instead refuses to obey him.

God is Living

Israel lived in a world that believed in many gods. The Old Testament writers mocked these gods as being nothing and they proclaimed Yahweh as the only living God. In contrast to the idols who can do nothing, "Yahweh is the true God; he is the living God, the eternal King" (Jer 10:10). The test on Mount Carmel proved to the people that Yahweh —not Baal— is the living God. The people shouted, "Yahweh, he is God! Yahweh, he is God!" (1 Kgs 18:39).[1]

As the living God, Yahweh is the source of life. "As surely as Yahweh lives, who has given us breath," was the testimony of one king (Jer 38:16). As a living God, Yahweh acts. God said of the same king,

---

[1]Translations of Scripture are based on the *New International Version*, modified when necessary to get at the original meaning of the text. In many translations, "Yahweh" is translated as "the LORD."

"As surely as I live, he shall die in Babylon" (Ezek 17:16). But the same living God desires repentance: "As surely as I live, I take no pleasure in the death of the wicked" (Ezek 33:11).

The living God is everlasting. "O Yahweh, are you not from everlasting?" (Hab 1:12). The Psalmist testifies: "from everlasting to everlasting you are God" (Ps 90:2). God has no beginning and no end. He is eternal.

In contrast to pagan polytheism, there is only one God in the Old Testament. Israel's confession of faith was: "Hear, O Israel, Yahweh, our God, Yahweh is one" (Deut 6:4).

God is Personal

The living God is a person. He has many of the personal qualities that you and I have; or, since we are created in God's image, we have many of God's qualities.

Therefore, "God speaks (Gen 1:3), hears (Ex 16:12), sees (Gen 6:12), smells (1 Sam 26:19), laughs (Ps 2:4) and whistles (Is 7:18)"; God "has eyes (Amos 9:4), hands (Ps 139:5), arms (Is 51:9), ears (Is 22:14) and feet (Nah 1:3)."[2] Yet this language is anthropomorphic. In other words, human concepts are used to describe God. As a spirit, God does not have physical eyes or ears; but as a person, God can certainly see and hear.

God also has personal emotions. He feels "joy (Zeph 3:17), disgust (Lev 20:23), repentance (Gen 6:6) and jealousy (Ex 20:5)."[3] He loved Israel (Ezek 16:8) and was angry when they rejected him (Amos 1:2). God was also grieved and sad when his bride became a prostitute (Jer 3:14).

---

[2]E. Jacob, *Theology of the Old Testament*, p. 39.
[3]E. Jacob, *Theology of the Old Testament*, p. 40.

God is Absolutely Sovereign

Even though God is personal, he is absolutely transcendent. Moses and the Israelites sang, "Who among the gods is like you, O Yahweh? Who is like you, majestic in holiness, awesome in glory, working wonders?" (Ex 15:11). The Psalmist too asks this rhetorical question, "Who is like you, O Yahweh?" (Ps 35:10; 113:5). The answer to this rhetorical question is that there is no one like Yahweh.

This belief is also expressed in statement form. Moses performed miracles so that Pharaoh might know that "there is no one like Yahweh our God" (Ex 8:10). At the end of his life Moses proclaimed that "there is no one like the God of Jeshurun" (Deut 33:26). The psalmist also confesses that "among the gods there is none like you, O Yahweh" (Ps 86:8).

The Old Testament shows to us a God who is utterly majestic and glorious. He is greater than any person or any other god. For God, "the nations are like a drop in a bucket; they are like dust on the scales." Thus, "to whom then will you compare God? What image will you compare him to?" (Is 40:15,18)

This God does whatever pleases him. "Our God is in heaven; he does whatever pleases him" (Ps 115:3). He has absolute power. After the crossing of the Red Sea, the Israelites sang, "Yahweh is my strength and song. . . . Your right hand, O Yahweh, was majestic in power" (Ex 15:2,6). God said to the childless Abraham and Sarah, "Is anything too hard for Yahweh?" (Gen 18:14). Nothing is too hard for God since he has all power.

At the end of the book of Job, God reveals himself as greater than any other being. Yahweh is the one who laid the earth's foundation; he shut up the sea behind the doors; he was the one who gave orders to the morning; he knows the springs of the oceans and the source of light and the storehouses of the snow; and he binds the stars together.

He knows everything about the mountain goats, the wild donkeys, the ostriches and the birds of the sky. He even understands the mysterious behemoth and leviathan (Job 38-41).

The glory of God is a manifestation of his majesty. When the thunder or voice of God is heard, all in God's temple cry, "Glory!" (Ps 29:9). To the Israelites the glory of Yahweh on Mount Sinai looked like a consuming fire (Ex 24:17). To Ezekiel the glory of Yahweh was a vision of fire and lights and cherubim and moving wheels (Ezek 1).

One author speaks of God's transcendence: "Yahweh is incomparable! There is none like Yahweh!" God has "unlimited sovereignty" and "incomparable power."[4] Indeed, there is no one like Yahweh.

God is Compassionate

The remarkable thing about the God of the Old Testament is that he is both transcendent and immanent. God is enthroned in heaven but he also comes down to help us. Just as God in the New Testament took flesh and became man, so Yahweh stoops down to meet our needs. In this respect, he is radically different from the pagan gods.

The psalmist indeed asks, "Who is like you, O Yahweh?" But he continues: "You rescue the poor from those too strong for them, the poor and needy from those who rob them" (Ps 35:10). The pagan gods do not show such a radical concern for the poor, so Yahweh is totally different from them.

The psalmist again says, "Who is like Yahweh our God, the One who sits enthroned on high," but also the one "who stoops down to look on the heavens and the earth" (Ps 113:5-6). Does Marduk stoop down to rescue the poor and needy? Does Baal rescue the poor from their enemies? Does the Muslim God come down and take

---

[4]W. Brueggemann, *Theology of the Old Testament*, pp. 206, 268.

human flesh? Only Yahweh, who is enthroned in heaven, is radically concerned for the poor and needy.

At the dedication of the temple, Solomon says that "there is no God like you in heaven above or on earth below—you who keep your covenant of love with your servants" (1 Kgs 8:23). God's otherness is seen in his love for his people.

Psalm 145 proclaims the greatness of Yahweh ("Great is Yahweh") but also his goodness ("Yahweh is gracious and compassionate, slow to anger and rich in love"). God is great and powerful, but his power is used for redemptive purposes. God acts in history to save his people.

One writer spoke of the tension between God's "unlimited sovereignty and risky solidarity."[5] God is the Creator of the world, and yet he is in solidarity with a weak and sinful nation, Israel. Surely his covenant relation with the people of Israel involved an enormous risk, the risk of repeated rejection. Yet God entered into this relationship because of love.

God is King

The entire Old Testament presupposes the kingship of God. Yahweh, not Marduk, is the great king. The kingship of Yahweh is a central theme of the Old Testament, or, perhaps the main idea in the Hebrew Scriptures.

What is said of the Psalms is true of the whole Old Testament:

> The gravitational center of life but also of history and of the whole creation is God. He is the Great King over all, the One to whom all things are subject. . . . As the Great King on whom all creatures depend, he opposes the "proud." . . . As the Great

---

[5]W. Brueggemann, *Theology of the Old Testament*, p. 268.

King over all the earth, the Lord has chosen Israel to be his
servant people.

> —J. Stek, "Introduction to Psalms" in *NIV Study Bible.*

The Psalms praise this Great King.

How awesome is Yahweh Most High, the great King over all
the earth! . . . God reigns over the nations; God is seated on his
holy throne

> —Ps 47:2, 8

Psalms 93, 97 and 99 open with the confession that "Yahweh reigns."
Since Yahweh is "the great King above all gods," we should worship
him "for he is our God and we are the people of his pasture" (Ps 95:3,6).

The Exodus experience reminded Israel that "Yahweh will reign
for ever and ever" (Ex 15:18). God's kingship is majestic in glory; but
his kingship is seen in his rescue of his people.

At the beginning of his ministry, Isaiah saw a vision of "the King,
Yahweh of hosts" (Is 6:5). Later in the same book God is called "Israel's
King and Redeemer" (Is 44:6). This is the King who would redeem
Israel from Babylon and bring them back to their land.

The Old Testament portrays God as a transcendent living King
who comes down in love to his people.

Study Questions

1. Describe the context of Jeremiah's assertion (Jer 10:10) that God is living.
2. How is anthropomorphic language used to describe the personal God?
3. Describe the sovereignty of God in Job 38-41.
4. Describe the greatness of God in Psalm 145.
5. Do you think the kingship of God is the central ideal of the Old Testament? Why or why not?

CHAPTER 2

THE NAME OF GOD

In the Old Testament, God has various names or titles. Some are generic, but one is personal.

Every culture has a common name or title for God because every culture has a belief in a creator God. Allah, Chukwu, Olodumare, Aondo and Na'an are all generic names for God.

El

One generic name for God in the Old Testament is "El." This word is related etymologically to the Arabic and Hausa "Allah." It is assumed that the word "El" conveys the idea of power. "What is powerful is divine."[1]

"El" is used only 238 times in the Old Testament. Sometimes it is used in a compound form. In Genesis we find "El Elyon" or God Most High (Gen 14:18-20); "El Roi" or the God who sees (Gen 16:13); "El Shaddai" or God Almighty (Gen 17:1); and "El Olam" or the everlasting God (Gen 21:33).

A related word for God is *Eloah*. This word, which is found 57 times in the Old Testament, is used mostly in the book of Job (e.g., Job 3:4,23; 4:9).

---

[1] E. Jacob, *Theology of the Old Testament*, p. 44.

Elohim

The common generic name for God is "Elohim." This word is used about 2570 times in the Old Testament. It is translated into our Bibles as God, Allah, Olodumare or the like.

The Old Testament opens with the words: "In the beginning Elohim created the heavens and the earth" (Gen 1:1). Almost every culture believes that God created the heavens and the earth. This is the belief in the creator God.

While the word "El" is singular, the word "Elohim" has a plural form but a singular meaning. Thus, Genesis 1:1 says that Elohim (plural form) created (singular verb) the heavens and earth. So why is "Elohim" in the plural form?

Some people think that the plural form of Elohim refers to the Trinity in the Old Testament. But it is more likely that the plural form Elohim reflects a plurality of majesty or intensity.[2] It is noteworthy that in some African cultures, when a king or chief speaks, he uses the plural "we." Also, when a subject speaks to the chief, the plural pronoun is used. (We can also think of the king or queen of England who uses the plural pronoun in reference to himself or herself. Queen Victoria once said of herself, "We are not amused.")

In the book of Jonah, the pagan sailors called on their god (*elohim*) and the pagan captain told Jonah to call on his god (*elohim*) (Jon 1:5-6). Elohim is a generic name for God.

Yahweh

But the personal name for God is the tetragrammaton (four letters), "Yahweh." This is the most common name for God, used 6828 times. Ultimately, the God of the Old Testament has only one name,

---

[2] H.D. Preuss, *Old Testament Theology* 1:147.

"Yahweh." Marduk, the god of Babylon, has fifty names, but the God of Israel has only one personal name.[3]

"Yahweh" is God's personal name revealed to Israel.[4] This name was revealed to Moses at the burning bush. There God promised to deliver his people from slavery. But Moses wanted to know God's name to tell the people. So God said,

> I am who I am. . . . Yahweh, the God of your fathers . . . has sent me to you. This is my name forever, the name by which I am to be remembered from generation to generation.
>
> —Ex 3:14-15

This was probably not the first revelation of Yahweh's name to his people. Already during the time of Adam's son Seth, people "began to call on the name of Yahweh" (Gen 4:26). Abram built altars to Yahweh and "called on the name of Yahweh" (Gen 12:8; 13:4). But the revelation of Yahweh's name to Moses was a significant event at the beginning of Israel's history.[5]

The meaning of "Yahweh" is not completely clear but there seems to be a connection between the Hebrew words for "I am" and "Yahweh." The name Yahweh conveys the idea of presence: God was present with Israel in their slavery, and he would be with them during their suffering and in their liberation.

Yahweh is then God's special name for his people Israel. It is his covenant name. It is the special name revealed to his people.

---

[3]H.D. Preuss, *Old Testament Theology*, 1:140.

[4]Traditionally, Yahweh was translated as "Jehovah." Scholars today think that Yahweh was the original pronunciation.

[5]In reference to Ex. 6:3, William Dyrness says that "God is not insisting on a completely new name, but a new understanding of his presence that will come to be associated with this name" (*Themes in Old Testament Theology*, p. 33).

In the story of Jonah, the sailors first knew only Elohim. But then Jonah finally made his confession, "I am a Hebrew and I worship Yahweh, the God of heaven, who made the sea and the land" (Jon 1:9). After that the sailors started praying to Yahweh. They "greatly feared Yahweh and they offered a sacrifice to Yahweh and made vows to him" (Jon 1:16). The sailors were now believers in Yahweh.

It is unfortunate that in our Bible translations the personal name of Yahweh is often concealed. Many English translations have "the LORD" for Yahweh. In Hausa the word "Ubangiji" translates Yahweh. But we should not forget the significance of God's personal name.

Sometimes Yahweh is combined with the word for armies or hosts: Yahweh Sabaoth or Yahweh of hosts.[6] This term is found about 261 times in the Old Testament. God is the Lord of the heavenly and earthly armies.

David said to Goliath, "I come against you in the name of Yahweh of hosts, the God of the armies of Israel" (1 Sam 17:45). The term is found frequently in Haggai, Zechariah and Malachi. For example, it is Yahweh of hosts who promises to shake the heavens and earth, the sea and the dry land and all nations (Hag 2:6-7).

Yahweh is God's special name for his people. It tells us that God is present with us. This God will keep his covenant promises.

---

[6]The NIV usually has "the LORD Almighty" for "Yahweh of hosts."

Study Questions

1. What is the translation of Elohim and Yahweh in English? What is the translation of Elohim and Yahweh in your language?
2. Why is Elohim in the plural form? Are there any analogies to this practice in your culture?
3. What is a possible meaning of Yahweh? Why was this important to the Israelites in Egyptian slavery?
4. What is the meaning of Yahweh Sabaoth? Which armies are being referred to?

CHAPTER 3

A HOLY AND LOVING GOD

As we look at God in the Old Testament, we are confronted with a Supreme Being who is both transcendent and immanent. Four characteristics or attributes of God in particular stand out.

The Holiness of God

In Isaiah's vision of God, the seraphim proclaimed: "Holy, holy, holy is Yahweh of hosts" (Is 6:3). Repeatedly in the Old Testament, God is said to be holy.

Holiness is a common concept in ancient religions. In traditional Africa, for example, there were shrines and other holy places which belonged to the gods and were thus off limits for the ordinary person.

The term "holy" is thus "synonymous with the divine."[1] A holy thing is something that belongs to God. The Hebrew root for holiness is *qadash*. It defines things that belong to God.

Holy things, belonging to God, are separated from ordinary life. Before God appeared to the people on Mount Sinai, Moses was told to "put limits around the mountain and set it apart as holy" (Ex 19:23). Later, the people were not allowed to enter into the temple and especially the Holy of Holies.

---

[1] E. Jacob, *Theology of the Old Testament*, p. 87.

God's holiness refers to his glory and majesty. God's holiness expresses his "radical otherness."[2] The book of Habakkuk pictures this holy God: "God came from Teman, the Holy One from Mount Paran. His glory covered the heavens and his praise filled the earth" (Hab 3:3).

This holy God does not tolerate sin or any breach of his holiness. When some people from Beth Shemesh looked into the ark of the covenant, God struck them down. Their compatriots then asked, "Who can stand in the presence of Yahweh, this holy God?" (1 Sam 6:20)

Isaiah pictures Israel's "Holy One" as a flame that burns and consumes disobedient nations (Is 10:17). In Ezekiel, God shows himself holy by punishing Sidon and Gog (Ezek 28:22; 38:16). The holy God will not tolerate sin.

Joshua challenged the people:

> You are not able to serve Yahweh. He is a holy God; he is a jealous God. He will not forgive your rebellion and your sins.
>
> —Josh 24:19

The holy God punishes sin; but it is surprising to see that God's holiness can also be God's acting in the favor of Israel or a believer. God's holiness is sometimes salvation for his people.

When Hannah received a baby, she praised God and said, "There is no one holy like Yahweh" (1 Sam 2:2). When the Israelites were delivered from Egypt, they praised God as being "majestic in holiness" (Ex 15:11). God's holiness during the Exodus was God's judgment on Pharaoh's army and his salvation for Israel.

Frequently in the second part of Isaiah, the "Holy One of Israel" is the Savior or Redeemer of Israel (e.g., Is 41:14; 43:3,14). God is the one who would redeem Israel from Babylonian captivity.

---

[2]W. Brueggemann, *Theology of the Old Testament*, p. 288.

Forgiveness is part of the nature of this holy God. In Hosea, we hear:

> I will not carry out my fierce anger, nor devastate Ephraim again, for I am God, and not man—the Holy One among you.
>
> —Hos 11:9

God's holiness then refers to his majesty but also his compassion. A remarkable verse brings these two elements together. God is "the high and lofty one . . . whose name is holy" and who lives "in a high and holy place." But this holy God is "also with the one who is contrite and lowly in spirit" (Is 57:15).3

God's holiness consists of his majesty; but his majesty is seen in his compassion for the humble and lowly.

The Justice of God

As a holy God, Yahweh always does what is right and just. Abraham asks the rhetorical question: "Will not the Judge of all the earth do right?" (Gen 18:25). Of course God always does what is just or right.

There are two Hebrew words for justice or righteousness. Both *tsedeq* and *mishpat* refer to something that is right or just.

There are two sides to God's justice: he punishes sinners and he saves the righteous. The psalmist proclaims: "Yahweh is righteous, he loves justice" (Ps 11:7). Practically this means that the wicked will be defeated and the righteous will be saved.

God's justice can come against Israel as well as the nations. Before the destruction of Jerusalem, Zephaniah proclaims that "Yahweh within her is righteous; he does no wrong: morning by morning he dispenses his justice" (Zeph 3:5). The destruction of Jerusalem because of her sins is an example of God's justice. Daniel, sitting in exile, recognized that "Yahweh our God is righteous in everything he does" and therefore Israel was punished for her sins (Dan 9:14).

But the miracle of God's grace is that his righteousness often meant salvation for his people. God was faithful to his covenant with his people and therefore he was righteous in saving them.

The psalmist who was saved from his enemies confessed, "Yahweh is righteous; he has cut me free from the cords of the wicked" (Ps 129:4). Again, "Yahweh is righteous in all his ways and loving toward all he has made" (Ps 145:17). "Yahweh is gracious and righteous; our God is full of compassion" (Ps 116:5).

When sinners stand before the just God, they might be afraid of God's justice. But often the psalmist longs for God's justice because this is salvation for him.

In Psalm 7, the psalmist, who is surrounded by his enemies, longs for God's justice. He prays, "Arise, Yahweh, in your anger . . . decree justice" (vs. 6). He knows that "God is a righteous judge, a God who expresses his wrath every day" (vs. 11). But he hopes that this "righteous God" will bring him salvation (vs. 9). God's justice here is judgment for the wicked and salvation for the righteous.

Thus God's acts of salvation can be called "righteous acts." When God delivered Deborah and Israel from the enemy, the singers celebrated "the righteous acts of Yahweh" (Judg 5:11).

God's promise of salvation for the exiles in Babylon is also an act of righteousness. God said, "I am bringing my righteousness near . . . and my salvation will not be delayed" (Is 46:13). The prophet often uses righteousness and salvation in poetic parallelism: for him they have the same meaning (see Is 45:8).

The Wrath of God

The wrath or anger of God is a manifestation of his justice. "Wrath is one of the most frequently mentioned of the feelings of God."[3]

------

[3]E. Jacob, *Theology of the Old Testament*, p. 114.

To the wicked, God is like a roaring lion. The wicked are not necessarily the other nations. Amos said to Israel, "Yahweh roars from Zion and thunders from Jerusalem" (Amos 1:2). God would send fire on both the pagan lands and the lands of Israel and Judah because of their sins (Amos 1:3-2:5).

God's wrath is a response to human sin.

> Always there is a correlation between the intensity of sin and of wrath: the graver the sin the fiercer will be the wrath; but the diminution of sin will weaken the wrath.
> —E. Jacob, *Theology of the Old Testament*, p. 116.

When Israel broke the covenant, she would face God's anger. Israel was warned not to worship idols, for God "is a jealous God and his anger will burn against you" (Deut 6:14-15; cf. 11:16-17). When a person violates the covenant, "God's wrath and zeal will burn upon that person" (Deut 29:20).

When Israel's sin had gone too far, God made Assyria "the rod of [his] anger" against Israel (Is 10:5). The day of Yahweh for Jerusalem would be "a day of wrath" and "a day of distress and anguish" (Zeph 1:15).

The nations too would experience God's wrath because they had violated God's moral order. Nahum says of Nineveh, "Yahweh is a jealous and avenging God; Yahweh takes vengeance and is filled with wrath" (Nah 1:2). Assyria's armies had brutally attacked many nations in violation of God's natural laws. Assyria and her capital Nineveh would suffer Yahweh's wrath.

Yet God is slow to anger and abundant in mercy. God revealed himself to Moses as

> Yahweh, Yahweh, the compassionate and gracious God, slow
> to anger, abounding in love and faithfulness, maintaining love
> to thousands, and forgiving wickedness, rebellion and sin.
>
> —Ex 34:6-7

Jonah knew that God was "a gracious and compassionate God, slow to anger and abounding in love" (Jon 4:2). So the king of Assyria repented, believing that God would "turn from his fierce anger" (Jon 3:9).

The psalmist said, "Yahweh is compassionate and gracious, slow to anger, abounding in love" (Ps 103:8). In another place, we are told that Yahweh's "anger lasts only a moment, but his favor lasts a lifetime" (Ps 30:5). But this is for those who are in a covenant relation with God.

The Love of God

The Old Testament teaches both the wrath of God and the love of God. A good theology will take both of these attributes seriously.

Twenty-six times Psalm 136 proclaims that "his love (*hesed*) endures forever." We see God's love through his "great wonders": the wonder of creation and the Exodus and the journey through the wilderness and the entry into the Promised Land (vss. 4-22). God's love is seen in his remembering our low estate and freeing us from the enemy (vss. 23-24).

The unique Hebrew word for God's love is *hesed*, sometimes translated as "mercy" or "lovingkindness." But the NIV "love" is the best translation. The end of Psalm 23 is best translated as: "Surely goodness and love will follow me all the days of my life" (Ps 23:6).

Usually *hesed* is God's covenant love toward his people.[4] In the Old Testament, God's love is directed especially towards Israel. God said, "When Israel was a child, I loved him" (Hos 11:1). Malachi opens with

---

[4]See E. Jacob, *Theology of the Old Testament*, p. 104.

the words, "I have loved Jacob" (Mal 1:2). In Isaiah, God reaffirms his love for Israel (Is 43:4).

The most profound metaphor for God's covenant love is marriage. Hosea shows the intimacy of this love. Hosea's love for the prostitute is an illustration of "the inexplicable and paradoxical character of God's love."[5]

Jeremiah reminds Israel of the time in the wilderness when she was God's bride (Jer 2:2). But now, God says with great sorrow, Israel has become a prostitute (Jer 2:20). Jeremiah portrays God as a husband who longs for his wife to return. "Return, faithless people for I am your husband," God pleads (Jer 3:14).[6] God's love for Israel continues even when they disobey.

Although God's love normally extends to Israel, sometimes it goes beyond God's chosen people. Isaiah says of the pagan king Cyrus, "Yahweh loves him" (Is 48:14; cf. RSV). One example of God's enduring love is his giving food to every creature (Ps 136:25).

The Old Testament God is thus holy and just and loving.

---

[5]W. Eichrodt, *Theology of the Old Testament*, 1:252.
[6]Abraham Heschel in *The Prophets* shows the pathos of God's love for Israel in Jeremiah and Hosea.

Study Questions

1. Define the Old Testament concept of holiness.
2. Describe God's holiness in 1 Samuel 2:1-2.
3. Describe the Old Testament concept of justice and righteousness.
4. Describe God's justice in Psalm 7.
5. When is God angry? When is God slow to anger?
6. How does Hosea's marriage to Gomer illustrate God's love?

CHAPTER 4

CREATION

The first act of the sovereign God in recorded history is creation. The Bible begins with the words, "In the beginning God created."

The book of Genesis contains two creation accounts: the first account gives the cosmic perspective (Gen 1:1-2:3); the second account is focused on Adam and Eve (Gen 2:4-25). These two accounts are complementary. They tell the story of creation from two different perspectives.

The biblical story of creation is polemical against the pagan religions. The Babylonians, for example, believed in 600 gods including the sun, moon and stars. But Genesis proclaims that all of these physical, natural objects were created by God. Instead of many gods, there is only one true God, whose name is Yahweh.

Genesis tells us that Yahweh is the King over the world. It is this Great King who created the world through the royal decrees found in the first chapter of the Bible. Yahweh is King; the other gods are just idols.

The Process of Creation

So, how was the universe created? The Old Testament does not answer all of our scientific questions. But a few things stand out.

First of all, Yahweh, the Supreme God, is the Creator. In this, Scripture agrees with many of our traditional religions. The Supreme God has many names: Allah, Chukwu, Oludumare; and it is this Supreme God who made everything that exists. The world did not evolve by itself, but the Supreme God is the one who made the world.

Secondly, creation was a process. Genesis identifies six days of creation. But before these six days there was a world that was "formless and empty" (Gen 1:2). Creation was partly the process of separation. God separated light from darkness, the water on the earth from the water in heaven, and the day from the night (Gen 1:4,6-7,14,18).

This happened in six days. We don't know how long these days were. Our 24-hour days are defined by the sun and the earth, but the sun was only created in the fourth day. The psalmist tells us that a thousand years in God's sight are like a single day. The day of Yahweh in the Old Testament is sometimes longer than a 24-hour day. How long were the days in Genesis?

It is interesting to note a parallelism between the first three days and the second three days. In the first day, light was created; in the fourth day, the sun and moon were made. In the second day, the heavens and seas were defined; in the fifth day, the birds and fish were made. In the third day, dry land appeared; in the sixth day, animals and humans were made. Should we take these days in chronological sequence or in pairs?

There are different views about the process of creation. But all Christians believe that it is the Supreme God who created. Yahweh and not Marduk is the Creator.

Third, there was no evil before creation. The second verse of the Bible tells us that the earth was "formless and empty" (*tohu wa bohu*). These words suggest a primeval chaos. But we reject the idea that there was a moral or spiritual chaos before creation. The chaos in this second verse is a physical formlessness and not a spiritual one. The formless and empty earth was the building material for God's creation. It was God who first made this formless earth.

The darkness and the waters at the beginning of Genesis are also not morally or ethically evil. Water and darkness were made by God and are good. While the Genesis story has similarities to the Babylonian creation story, there are qualitative differences. In the Babylonian religion, the waters were evil; but in the Bible the waters are created by God and are good.

To say that creation is salvation[1] is wrong. Salvation presupposes the existence of evil; but in the biblical doctrine of creation, evil had not yet appeared. Evil came into the world after creation. Before creation there was only God, and God is only good.

Finally, God's creation of the world was very good. The first chapter of Genesis concludes by saying that "God saw all that he had made, and it was very good" (Gen 1:31). There was no evil at that time.

Creation of "Adam"

The climax of God's creation is the human person. At the end of the sixth day, God made man and woman in his image.

The first creation account reports God's words: "Let us make *adam* in our image, in our likeness, and let *them* rule . . ." (Gen 1:26). *Adam* is here a generic term referring to both man and woman. This is the case in the next verse: "So God created the *adam* in his own image, in the image of God he created him; male and female he created *them*" (Gen 1:27).

---

[1]G. von Rad (*Old Testament Theology*, 1:139) calls creation "a saving work of Jahweh." Also, to say that creation is "an eschatological concept" (E. Jacob, *Theology of the Old Testament*, p. 148) is nonsense. Creation is at the beginning of cosmic history; eschatology is at the end of this history.

Only the *adam* is made in God's image and likeness. Man and woman are different from the animals since they are like God. We are able to think and reason like God; we are also able to love as God loves.

Then, God gave the *cultural mandate*:

> Be fruitful and multiply; fill the earth and subdue it. Rule over the fish of the sea and the birds of the air and over every living creature that moves on the ground.
>
> —Gen 1:28

Part of the image of God is our task to rule over the earth. God has given us the world to develop and to rule.

Care for the Earth

But too often in ruling we have destroyed the earth. We hunt species of animals until the species is extinct. We cut down trees without planting new ones. We pollute the land and the waters. How then should we rule the earth?

The second creation account answers this question. "Yahweh God took the *adam* and put him in the Garden of Eden to work it and take care of it" (Gen 2:15). A better translation might read: "to serve (*abad*) and to protect (*shamar*) the earth."[2]

Psalm 24 tells us that "the earth is Yahweh's and its fullness." If the earth belongs to God, then we are stewards of this earth. A steward takes care of something that belongs to his master. The earth belongs to God, so as stewards we should take care of this trust.

Continued Creation

In a sense God's creation continues today. Any time a baby is born, God is creating. Psalm 104 tells us about God's first creation and his

---

[2] T. Fretheim, *God and World in the Old Testament*, p. 53.

continuing creation. God "set the earth on its foundations; it can never be moved" (Ps 104:5). But God also "makes grass grow for the cattle and plants for man to cultivate" (Ps 104:14). All of creation depends on God's providence.

The last chapters of the book of Job also testify to God's providence. Only God knows how the mountain goats, the wild donkeys, the horses and the birds exist (Job 38-41). Only God cares for them.

God's creation is "very good" (Gen 1:31). Let us use and take care of this creation.

Study Questions

1. How is the Genesis creation account polemical against pagan religions?
2. How are the two creation accounts different?
3. Why is creation not salvation?
4. How does the cultural mandate apply to us today?
5. How can we care for the earth today?

CHAPTER 5

THE HUMAN PERSON

The human person is a paradoxical creature. On the one hand, we are like God himself. On the other hand, we are weak and "desperately corrupt" (Jer 17:9). We are capable of doing enormous good and terrible evil.

The Image of God

The book of Genesis tells us that *adam* or man is made in the image or likeness of God (Gen 1:26-27). This means that we are like God and different from the animals. Human beings have the ability to reason and to love on a totally different level than the animals. In many respects we are like God.

The next verse in Genesis gives us an example of this likeness. Adam was given the authority and mandate to rule over the rest of creation: "Be fruitful and multiply; fill the earth and subdue it" (Gen 1:28).

The psalmist sings of man's glory.

> What is man that you are mindful of him, the son of man that you care for him? You have made him a little lower than God, and crowned him with glory and honor
>
> —Ps 8:4-5

The creation stories tell us that man and woman were placed in a threefold relationship. They were created in a good relationship to God, to each other and to the world.[1]

First, the man and woman were in fellowship with God. The Genesis story pictures God walking in the garden, communing with Adam and Eve. Man and woman in their original state were in perfect harmony with God.

Second, the man and woman lived in love with each other. The story of their sin suggests a perfect harmony before they fell. This reminds us of the social dimension of humanity.

Third, man was in a good relation with the created world. *Adam* was to "rule over the fish of the sea and the birds of the air and over every living creature that moves on the ground" (Gen 1:28). But this ruling was not to be exploitation. In the second creation story, God placed the *adam* in the garden "to work it and take care of it" (Gen 2:15).

But sin ruined this threefold relationship. When Adam and Eve disobeyed God, they felt guilty and shameful before God. The man and woman blamed each other for the curse that had come on them. The land was cursed because of them.

The story of redemption in the Old Testament speaks of a restoration of the threefold relationship. Micah looks forward to the time when "the mountain of Yahweh's temple will be established" and many nations will stream to it. There God "will teach us his ways." There will be peace between nations:

> Nation will not take up sword against nation, nor will they
> train for war any more. Every one will sit under his own vine
> and under his own fig tree, and no one will make them afraid.
>
> —Mic 4:1-4; cf. Is 2:2-4

------

[1]See A. Hoekema, *Created in God's Image*, pp. 75-96; W. Dyrness, *Themes in Old Testament Theology*, pp. 79-84.

Isaiah tells us that

> The wolf will live with the lamb, the leopard will lie down with
> the goat, the calf and the lion and the yearling together.
>
> —Is 11:6

These prophecies refer to the kingdom of the Messiah that was fulfilled
in Jesus Christ. In the Messiah the threefold relation is being restored.

Terminology for the Human Person

The Old Testament has different terms to describe the human person.
Most of these words are used in parallel fashion. There is thus a
"stereometric" use of these terms: in other words, these terms have
overlapping meaning.[2]

An example is found in the Psalms: "My soul yearns . . . for the
courts of Yahweh; my heart and my flesh cry out for the living God"
(Ps 84:2). Here the soul, heart and flesh are different ways of referring
to a person.

We will consider a few of these terms.

Flesh

The word "flesh" (*basar*) conveys the weakness and mortality of a
person.

Sometimes flesh refers to the physical part of the human body.
After God removed a rib from Adam's body, he "closed up the place
with flesh" (Gen 2:21). Satan attacked Job's "flesh and bones" (Job 2:5).
Flesh can also refer to the meat of animals (Lev 7:15-21).

Often, though, flesh refers to mortal man. "All flesh is grass," says
the prophet (Is 40:6). We will quickly fade away like the flower.

---

[2]H.W. Wolff, *Anthropology of the Old Testament*, pp. 7-9.

The arm of the great King Sennacherib is "only the arm of flesh" in comparison to God's power (2 Chr 32:8). The horses of the Egyptians "are flesh and not spirit" (Is 31:3); in other words, they are weak before God's power.

Sometimes flesh is sinful humanity. Before the flood, God said that he would not contend with man forever "for he is flesh" (Gen 6:3). God saw that "all flesh had corrupted their way upon the earth." So God resolved "to destroy all flesh" (Gen 6:12,17).

Yet, the flesh can also represent the human person that desires God. The psalmist says that his "heart and flesh cry out for the living God" (Ps 84:2). Again, the psalmist's flesh trembles in fear of God (Ps 119:120).

Flesh, then, refers to the weak and physical side of a person.

"Soul"

Traditionally the word *nephesh* has been translated as "soul." But *nephesh* usually refers to the life of a person or the person himself.

God said to Satan that he could touch Job's body but that he must spare Job's *nephesh* or life (Job 2:6). The Mosaic law specified "life for life" in the case of serious injury (Ex 21:23).

In the creation story, a living *nephesh* is a living being. The waters and land brought forth living creatures (Gen 1:20,21,24). Then God created the *adam* and he became a living being, not a living soul (Gen 2:7).

Often, *nephesh* simply refers to the whole person. When Jacob went to Egypt to see Joseph, he went with 66 persons, not 66 souls (Gen 46:26). Altogether, 70 persons went to Egypt (Gen 46:27).

The psalmist in his whole being longs for and praises God. "I [my soul] thirst for God" (Ps 42:2). "Praise Yahweh, my being" is his call to worship (Ps 103:1).

Nephesh should not be seen as a separate part of the human person as the Greek philosophers viewed it. Instead, *nephesh* usually is the whole person.

Spirit

The spirit (*ruach*) is the non-physical part of a person. We *are* living souls, but we *have* human spirits.[3]

The Bible distinguishes between God's Spirit and the human spirit. The divine Spirit creates the human spirit. The human spirit is "the organ of our psychic life."[4] The human spirit is "a psychological reality residing in man and . . . able to be the seat of faculties and desires."[5] Many of our emotions and desires come from our spirit.

Rebecca and Isaac felt "a bitterness of spirit" when their son Esau married pagan wives (Gen 26:35). But when Jacob learned that his son Joseph was still alive, "his spirit revived" (Gen 45:27).

The Preacher contrasts the patient spirit with the proud spirit, and he warns against an angry spirit (Eccl 7:8-9).

After the exile, God stirred up the spirit of Zerubbabel and the spirit of Joshua and the spirit of the people, causing them to build the temple (Hag 1:14).

The psalmist prayed for "a willing spirit," and he reminded us that "the sacrifices of God are a broken spirit and a contrite heart" (Ps 51:12,17).

The human spirit, then, is the seat of emotions and religious feelings.

---

[3]E. Jacob, *Theology of the Old Testament*, pp. 158, 161.
[4]W. Dyrness, *Themes in Old Testament Theology*, p. 86.
[5]E. Jacob, *Theology of the Old Testament*, p. 162.

Heart

Heart is the most frequent designation for the human person. The Hebrew *leb* and *lebab* are used about 850 times in the Old Testament.

In the first place, the heart is the central physical organ of a person. But the Bible was written in a pre-scientific time, so the heart is somewhat analogous to the mind of a person.

An example of this pre-scientific thinking is the story of Abigail and Nabal. We learn that Nabal's heart died at the hearing of news about David, but ten days later Nabal himself died (1 Sam 25:37-38).

The heart is the central organ of a person. Aaron's breastplate was over his heart (Ex 28:29-30). Joab cast three spears into Absalom's heart, eventually leading to his death (2 Sam 18:14).

But usually the heart is the psychological, emotional and spiritual center of a person. The book of Proverbs talks of a glad heart and the sorrow of heart (Prov 15:13). The psalmist speaks of the desire of one's heart (Ps 21:2).

Often the heart is "the seat of religious knowledge."[6] It is the religious center of a person. It can be directed to God or away from him.

Sometimes the heart is hardened against God. We read in Exodus that Pharaoh's heart was hardened (Ex 7:22; 8:15). This means that he opposed the works of God.

The fool said in his heart that there is no God (Ps 14:1). Even Israel did not always have an understanding heart (Deut 29:4). Jeremiah complains that the heart is deceitful above all things (Jer 17:9).

But the heart can be changed. God promised Israel "an undivided heart," "a new spirit" and "a heart of flesh" (Ezek 11:19). After the exile,

---

[6]E. Jacob, *Theology of the Old Testament*, p. 165.

God would replace their "heart of stone" with a "heart of flesh" (Ezek 36:26).

The Old Testament sees the human person as a unity. A person is to love God in his entire being. The Shema said: "Love Yahweh your God with all your heart and with all your person [soul] and with all your strength" (Deut 6:5).

Study Questions

1. How do you think that we are in the image of God?
2. Describe the three-fold relationship that we are created in.
3. What is the meaning of "flesh" in the Old Testament?
4. Compare the meanings of "soul" and "spirit."
5. What is a person's heart in the Old Testament?

CHAPTER 6

EVIL

God created the world good. At the end of creation, God saw everything that he had made, and it was "very good" (Gen 1:31). But it is a sad fact that our world is full of evil. So what is evil in the Old Testament? Where did this evil come from?

The basic Hebrew word for evil is *ra*. *Ra* is anything that is bad. *Ra*, or that which is bad, is the opposite of *tov*, or that which is good.

In the Garden of Eden, there was a tree of the knowledge of good (*tov*) and evil (*ra*) (Gen 2:9). Amos teaches Israel to seek good (*tov*) and not evil (*ra*) (Amos 5:14). But in Pharaoh's dream, we find cows that are both fat and evil (*ra*) (Gen 41:3). An evil thing is something that is not good.

There are two kinds of evil in the Old Testament: moral evil and natural evil. Moral evil is a sinful act; natural evil is a disaster or calamity.[1]

Moral Evil

Often evil in the Old Testament is a sinful act. Repeatedly the Israelites did evil in the sight of God (e.g. Judg 2:11; 3:7,12; 4:1). Their kings also frequently did evil or sinned (e.g. 2 Kgs 15:9,18,24,28). At the time of

---

[1] The NIV often translates natural evil as "disaster."

Jonah, the evil of Nineveh came to God's notice (Jon 1:2). Evil in these cases refers to human sin.

So where did the first human sin or evil come from? The book of Genesis gives this account.

The second chapter of Genesis tells of the tree of the knowledge of good and evil (Gen 2:9). But the *knowledge* of evil is not the same as evil. At that point, there was a *possibility* of evil; but evil was not present in the Garden.

The third chapter of Genesis describes how Adam and Eve ate of the fruit of the tree in disobedience to God. This is the first human sin. This is the origin of human evil.

Adam and Eve were created good and with a free will. They were free to choose between good and evil. At the critical testing point, though, they made the wrong choice. They chose evil instead of good. They sinned. This is the origin of human sin.

Of course, they were tempted by the serpent to do evil. Satan was a spiritual being who had the freedom to do good or evil. The New Testament suggests that Satan fell when he chose evil at the beginning of time.

Moral evil comes from our heart. Although Satan may tempt us, in the end the source of evil is the human heart. We are ultimately responsible for our actions. We should not blame God or Satan for our personal sins.

Sin

Sin is now an integral part of human existence. At the time of the flood, God saw that "every inclination of the thoughts of the human heart was only evil all the time" (Gen 6:5). Jeremiah testified that "the heart is deceitful above all things and desperately corrupt" (Jer 17:9).

A key word for sin is *pasha* (to rebel) or *pesha* (rebellion). In history, Moab rebelled against Israel (2 Kgs 1:1). The same word is used by Isaiah to describe Israel's sin against Yahweh: "they have rebelled against me" (Is 1:2).

One commentator said that this is "the Old Testament's most profound word for 'sin,' indicating its theological meaning as 'revolt against God.'"[2]

The essence of sin is rebellion against God. David in a prayer to God realized that it was "against you, you only, have I sinned" (Ps 51:4).

A second word for sin is *hata*, which means "to miss the mark" or "to sin." (This word is also used in Judges 20:16 of men who would not miss the target with their sling.)

This word suggests that sin is missing the mark or failing to obey God's law. The noun "indicates spiritual and moral failure."[3] The measure of such failure is the Torah.

A third word for sin, *asham,* emphasizes the guilt of the sinner. The Torah says: "A person who sins and does what is forbidden in any of Yahweh's commands is guilty and will be held responsible" (Lev 5:17).

In the Torah a person is guilty both from sin and impurity. The law states that if a person touches something that is ceremonially unclean, "he has become unclean and is guilty" (Lev 5:2).

Human sin results in divine punishment. The oracles of judgment against the nations show that even the peoples who do not know the Torah are held accountable. But Israel, which had the Torah, was particularly responsible. God said to Israel, "You only have I known of all the families of the earth; therefore I will punish you for your sins" (Amos 3:2).

---

[2] S.J De Vries, "Sin, Sinner," in *Interpreter's Dictionary of the Bible* 4:361.
[3] S.J. De Vries, "Sin, Sinner," in *IDB* 4:361.

Natural Evil

In addition to moral evil, there is natural evil. Evil in this sense is something that is physically bad.

The cows in Pharaoh's dream were not sinful, but they were gaunt and thus bad (Gen 41:3). Job had evil or painful sores on his body (Job 2:7). The storm striking Jonah's ship is called an evil (or calamity) (Jon 2:7-8).

God is often the cause of such evil. God said: "I form the light and create darkness; I bring *shalom* and create evil (ra)" (Is 45:7). Evil here is "disaster"—perhaps military defeat for Babylon, which would mean salvation for the Jews.

Evil or disaster also comes on God's people when they are not faithful. Before the fall of Samaria, God said: "When evil comes to a city, has not Yahweh caused it?" (Amos 3:6). Then God explains how he sent famine, drought, disease, plagues and defeat to Israel so that they would return to him (Amos 4:6-11). Natural evils struck Israel because she was morally evil.

The book of Jeremiah tells of the evil that would come on Judah because of her evil (sin). Because Judah had evil hearts, God would bring evil (or disaster) on her (Jer 11:8,11). God decreed evil on Judah because they had done evil (Jer 11:17). The Babylonian captivity was a natural evil that God had decreed because of the moral evil that Israel committed.

Often in the Old Testament it is God who causes disasters as a punishment for human sin. Natural evil is often—but not always—a consequence of moral evil.

Study Questions

1. What are the two basic meanings of the Hebrew word ra?
2. What is the origin of moral evil?
3. Why did God cause evil in Amos 3:6?
4. Why did God cause evil in Isaiah 45:7?
5. How is natural evil often a consequence of moral evil?

CHAPTER 7

SPIRITS

The ancient world, like the African world, believed in the existence of spirits. There is a wide range of spirits in the Old Testament.

The Hebrew word for spirit is *ruah,* which is also the word for wind or breath. There is a mysterious quality to the wind. One cannot see the wind, but one can feel its power. After the flood, God sent a *ruah* or wind over the earth and the waters receded (Gen 8:1). When Moses stretched out his hand over the sea, God drove the sea back with a strong east *ruah* (Ex 14:21).

The word *ruah* can also mean breath. In the traditional Hebrew mind, breath was associated with life. The flood story speaks of animals having the *ruah* or breath of life (Gen 6:17). At the exodus, the waters were driven back by the breath (*ruah*) of God's nostrils (Ex 15:8).

The wind and breath are impersonal; but *ruah* can also refer to a personal spirit. We have already considered the human spirit as a part of a man or woman. We will here look at the Spirit of God, good and evil spirits, and ancestral spirits.

The Spirit of God

The Spirit of God is the life-giving power of God. We see this power in creation and in salvation history.

The second verse of the Bible tells us that "the Spirit of God was hovering over the waters" (Gen 1:2). The psalmist says that God by his Spirit creates new life and renews the face of the earth (Ps 104:30). God's Spirit creates and sustains physical life.

But God's Spirit was also active in the redemptive history of Israel. God's Spirit helped Bezalel build the tabernacle (Ex 31:3; 35:31). The Spirit came on seventy elders and they prophesied (Num 11:17-29).

In the book of Judges, the Spirit of Yahweh came on Othniel (3:10), Gideon (6:34), Jephthah (11:29) and Samson (13:25; 14:6,19; 15:14), and they saved God's people.

Later, the Spirit of God came on Saul and he prophesied (1 Sam 10:6,10). But then the Spirit of Yahweh left Saul and came on David in power (1 Sam 16:13-14).

The Spirit of God empowered prophets to prophesy. The earlier prophets spoke through God's Spirit (Zech 7:12). The Spirit of Yahweh enabled one prophet to preach good news to the poor (Is 61:1). Micah was empowered by the Spirit to show Israel their sin (Mic 3:8). The Spirit showed Ezekiel visions (Ezek 8:3; 11:1).

But in the new messianic kingdom, God's Spirit would be poured out on every believer (Joel 2:28-29). God promised to give his people a "new heart" and a "new spirit." This would happen when God would put his Spirit in them (Ezek 36:26-27; 39:29).

God's Spirit then is the source of both physical and spiritual life.

Heavenly Spirits

As king, Yahweh has a heavenly court with heavenly spirits around him.[1]

In the book of Job, God is seated in heaven and the "sons of God" presented themselves before Yahweh (Job 1:6). At another time, the

---

[1] See H. D. Preuss, *Old Testament Theology*, 1:256-58.

prophet Micaiah "saw Yahweh sitting on his throne with all the host (or army) of heaven standing around him." From this host a "spirit" performed a task for God (1 Kgs 22:19,21-23).

We assume that these sons of God and the host of heaven are angels. One psalm calls on the angels, the mighty ones, the hosts and God's servants to praise Yahweh (Ps 103:20-21). Another psalm calls on the angels, the host, the sun, moon and stars to praise God (Ps 148:2-3). God is surrounded by many spiritual beings.

The prophet Isaiah had a vision of "the King, Yahweh of hosts" (Is 6:5). In this vision, God was surrounded by heavenly beings called seraphim. The seraphim, which we find only in Isaiah's vision, have the task of praising God.

The prophet Ezekiel had a vision of God surrounded by four living creatures or cherubim. (One of the living creatures is called a "spirit" in Ezekiel 1:20.) God's throne was above the cherubim (Ezek 10:1-2).

The cherubim are winged creatures who guard the heavenly throne and the tree of life. We find the cherubim at the Garden of Eden, guarding the tree of life (Gen 3:24). Two cherubim were over the ark of the covenant, providing God with his earthly throne. Four cherubim traveled with God in Ezekiel's vision. The cherubim "are the symbol of Yahweh's presence" and they "illustrate divine majesty."[2]

The angels are a general category of spiritual beings. The Hebrew word *malak* comes from the word "to send." Angels are often messengers of God. Jacob had a vision of angels going up and down the stairway or ziggurat of God (Gen 28:12).

The angel of Yahweh is an angel closely related to the person of God himself. The angel of Yahweh appeared to people like Hagar, Abraham, Moses, Balaam, Gideon and Elijah. The angel of Yahweh stopped Abraham from killing his son; this angel also appeared to

---

[2]H.D. Preuss, *Old Testament Theology*, 1:257.

Moses at the burning bush (Gen 22:11-15; Ex 3:2). It was this angel that led Israel out of Egypt and into the Promised Land (Ex 14:19; 23:23).

God's angels protected his people. The psalmist says:

> He will command his angels concerning you to guard you in all your ways; they will lift you up in their hands so that you will not strike your foot against a stone.
>
> —Ps 91:11-12

Satan

It is surprising to find only a few references to Satan in the Old Testament. The word "satan" means "the accuser." Initially, Satan may have been "a heavenly prosecutor within the court of Yahweh and under his direction."[3]

Thus, "the Satan" or the accuser brought charges against Job (Job 1-2). Again, "the Satan" brought charges against Joshua the high priest (Zech 3:1-2). In both cases, the men of God were acquitted.

But in the post-exilic book of Chronicles, Satan becomes the personal name of this evil spirit. There Satan tempts David to count the people of Israel (1 Chr 21:1).

Satan is not named in the temptation of Adam and Eve. But the New Testament says that Satan was "the ancient serpent" who deceived Adam and Eve (Rev 12:9).

Evil Spirits

Again, it is surprising to find so few references to evil spirits in the Old Testament. Perhaps the focus on the majesty of Yahweh pushed the evil spirits to the side.

---

[3]H.D. Preuss, *Old Testament Theology*, 1:260.

There are three main stories containing evil or harmful spirits. In each case, the spirit is an agent of God causing natural evil (*ra*) or confusion in order to punish or chastise a person or a group of persons.

When Abimelech and the town of Shechem killed the other sons of Gideon, God sent a harmful spirit on them to punish them (Judg 9:23). This evil or harmful spirit was doing God's just work.

After King Saul's disobedience, God sent a harmful spirit a few times to Saul (1 Sam 16:14; 18:10; 19:9). This spirit was in the service of God, following God's mysterious commands.

Finally, God sent a harmful spirit to King Ahab to lure him into battle and to his death (1 Kgs 22:21-23; 2 Chr 18:22-23). This spirit too was under God's direction.

These "evil spirits" were sent by God to punish disobedient individuals. They were not demons in the service of Satan. God sent them to do harmful things as a punishment for sin.

In Babylon there was a great preoccupation and fear of demons. But in the Old Testament there are only a few passing references to demons.

Lilith (Is 34:14) and Azalel (Lev 16:10) may have been demons in the traditional religion, but they were no longer a threat to the average Israelite. Only a couple of texts suggest that sacrifices were made to demons, who are equated with pagan idols (Deut 32:17; Ps 106:37-38).

While the opening pages of Mark's Gospel have frequent references to demons, the entire Old Testament has only "very sporadic and mostly minor statements about demons."[4]

Perhaps Satan and the demons were active behind the idolatry of the time. But the focus on the kingship of Yahweh seemed to push the demonic forces into the shadows.

---

[4]H.D. Preuss, *Old Testament Theology*, 1:259.

Ancestral Spirits

When a person dies, his spirit went to Sheol or the place of the dead. The Old Testament did not clearly distinguish between heaven and hell, as does the New Testament.

Sheol was a place of shadowy existence. The book of Isaiah dramatically pictures the descent of the King of Babylon into Sheol. At his death, this king travels to the world of the dead. The spirits or shadows (*rephaim*) of the dead greet this king (Is 14:9-12).

Once the spirit of Samuel was called out of the grave by a witch (1 Sam 28), but this was strongly condemned by the Torah. Necromancy was forbidden.

But there was hope for the believer. The psalmist believed that God would not abandon him to Sheol (Ps 16:10) but would redeem him from Sheol (Ps 49:15).

Enoch walked with God, and then God took him away (Gen 5:24). Elijah too was taken up to heaven in a whirlwind (2 Kgs 2:11).

Job believed that his Redeemer lives, and that at the end he would see God (Job 19:25-27).

The ancestral spirit of the believer would be with God. But the ancestral spirit of the unbeliever would remain in darkness.

Study Questions

1. What are the different possible meanings of ruaḥ?
2. What were the main functions of the Spirit of God in the Old Testament?
3. Describe three categories of heavenly spirits.
4. How was Satan an accuser in the Old Testament?
5. Why do you think there are so few references to Satan and the evil spirits in the Old Testament?
6. What would happen to an Old Testament believer when he or she died?

CHAPTER 8

ELECTION

The opening chapters of Genesis show the repeated sin and failure of mankind. First, Adam and Eve disobeyed God; then the whole world was found corrupt before God; then mankind built a tower in defiance of God.

This is the background for God's redemptive history. Election is a key part of this salvation history. Election is "the initial act by which Yahweh comes into relation with his people."[1]

The word elect (baḥar) means to choose. We often choose. We have elections to choose a President and a Governor. We choose a husband or wife. We choose a school or an occupation.

God's election is part of his plan of salvation. God chooses individuals and a people for redemptive purposes.

The Election of Abraham

After the repeated failure of mankind, God chose a man from Ur named Abram. Abram was elected for a special relationship and a special purpose. Abram would be blessed by God and he would be a blessing to others (Gen 12:1-3).

---

[1]E. Jacob, *Theology of the Old Testament*, p. 201.

The book of Nehemiah tells us that Yahweh God "chose Abram and brought him out of Ur of the Chaldeans and named him Abraham" (Neh 9:7). In Genesis, God said of Abraham, "I have known [loved] him" (Gen 18:19).

So why did God choose or love Abraham? He loved Abraham so that "all nations on earth will be blessed through him" (Gen 18:18). The next verse says that Abraham was known so that he and his children would do what is right and just (Gen 18:19).

Abraham was elected in order to be a blessing to the nations.

The Election of Israel

The election of Israel is a continuation of the election of Abraham, since Israel were his descendents.

The prophet Ezekiel describes this election with a story. Once there was a baby girl who was abandoned in a field, dirty and naked. But God passed by and saw the filthy infant and took her and washed her and clothed her. When the girl became a beautiful woman, God loved her and married her. He gave his wife beautiful clothes and jewelry and excellent food (Ezek 16:1-14).

This is a picture of Israel's election. Election is God's choosing and loving the people of Israel. So why did God choose Israel and not Egypt or Moab or Edom? This is a difficult question. Why did you choose your wife or husband and not someone else? Love cannot always be explained.

Moses tells Israel that "Yahweh your God has chosen you out of all the peoples of the earth to be his people, his treasured possession." But God did not love them because they were many or strong. Rather, "Yahweh loved you and kept the oath he swore to your forefathers" (Deut 7:6-8). Again,

> It is not because of your righteousness that Yahweh your God is giving you this good land to possess, for you are a stiff-necked people.
>
> —Deut 9:6

Election is about grace. When a handsome and wealthy man wants to marry you, this is grace. When someone pays your school fees, this is grace. When God chose and loved Israel, this too was grace.

There are two parts to election. Election entails privilege and responsibility.

Election entails *privilege*. In Amos, God says: "You only have I known [loved]" (Amos 3:2). In Deuteronomy, Moses announces that "Yahweh loved you" (Deut 7:8). In Exodus we read that Israel is God's "treasured possession" (Ex 19:5).

Election is about God's love and favor to one people. Israel in the Old Testament was more privileged than the nations around her.

But the chosen people had a special *responsibility*. Israel was God's treasured possession; therefore they were to be "a kingdom of priests and a holy nation" (Ex 19:6). They had the responsibility of being *holy* in the world.

The tragedy of ancient Israel is that they constantly failed. To continue the story of the prophet Ezekiel, the beautiful woman that God married eventually became a prostitute (Ezek 16:15-19). Spiritual adultery in the Old Testament is a metaphor for idolatry.

The prophet Amos expressed the privilege and responsibility of election well: "You only have I known of all the families of the earth; therefore I will punish you for all your sins" (Amos 3:2). Election for Israel was the privilege of being specially loved by God above all the nations; but it also meant punishment when they did not fulfill their responsibility. God's elect people were punished and taken off to Babylonian captivity because of their sins.

But even in captivity the Jews were God's chosen people. In the second part of Isaiah, God reassures "Jacob, whom I have chosen" that "I have chosen you and have not rejected you" (Is 41:8-9). God's chosen people would return from captivity. "Do not be afraid, O Jacob, my servant, Jeshurun, whom I have chosen," God said, for they would be restored (Is 44:2).

The election of Israel was a collective election. Israel as a group were loved and chosen. Even though the nation was chosen, not every individual in the nation was saved. The salvation of the people depended on their personal response to God.

The Election of Individuals

In the history of Israel, some significant individuals were chosen, often for special tasks.

We have seen that Abraham was chosen to be in a special relationship with God. Moses, the leader of God's people, was called God's "chosen one" (Ps 106:23).

Aaron the priest was the one whom God had chosen (Ps 105:26). Eli's father or ancestor was chosen to be God's priest in Israel (1 Sam 2:28). The priests and Levites too were chosen "to stand and minister in Yahweh's name always" (Deut 18:5).

In a similar way, certain kings were chosen to lead God's people. King Saul was called "the man Yahweh has chosen" (1 Sam 10:24). But when Saul proved unfaithful, God rejected him as king (1 Sam 15:23,26). The prophet Samuel then went to the house of Jesse where God chose David (1 Sam 16:8-12).

After the return from exile, God said that he had chosen the governor Zerubbabel (Hag 2:23). Probably he was a type of the chosen Messiah.

In one case a pagan king was chosen for a special task. The Persian emperor Cyrus was called God's anointed for the special assignment of returning the Jews back to the promised land (Is 45:1-6).

Conclusion

Although individual elections are significant in the Old Testament, the decisive election was that of Israel. God's plan of salvation in the Old Testament was centered on the election of Israel.

Today, the church is God's elect people. The church is the new Israel. Paul tells us that "not all who are descended from Israel are Israel" (Rom 9:6). The spiritual Israel are those who believe in Jesus Christ.

In his letter to the churches in Asia Minor, Peter said: "You are an elect people, a royal priesthood, a holy nation, a people belong to God" (1 Pet 2:9).

The church as the new Israel is now God's elect people.

Study Questions

1. What does the word election mean?
2. Why did God choose Abraham?
3. Why did God choose Israel?
4. What are the two parts of election as seen in Amos 3:2?
5. Why were Saul and David elected?
6. Does the election of Israel mean that God does not love the nations? Explain.

CHAPTER 9

COVENANT

In the last chapter, we saw that God elected Abraham and Israel out of grace. Abraham and Israel were elected to enter into a special relationship with God. This was grace.

In his relationship with his people, God made promises and agreements. These solemn agreements are called covenants.

The Hebrew word for covenant is *berith*. A covenant is "a solemn promise made binding by an oath, which may be either a verbal formula or a symbolic action."[1]

This chapter will look at significant Old Testament covenants. But first we should look at the Ancient Near Eastern context.

Ancient Near East Convenants

During the time of the exodus, the Hittite Empire flourished in Asia Minor. The Hittites had treaties or covenants to regulate political relations in the Empire.[2]

The basic treaty of the Hittite Empire was the *suzerain-vassal treaty*. This was a formal agreement between the great king (the "suzerain") and a smaller king (the "vassal"). The heart of this treaty was a political

---

[1] G. Mendenhall, "Covenant" in *Interpreter's Dictionary of the Bible* 1:714.
[2] See G. Mendenhall, "Covenant," in *IDB* 1:714-15.

relationship between two kings. The vassal promised to be loyal to the great king, and the great king promised to protect the vassal. Legal treaty documents were produced and kept in the temple of each king. The covenant was sworn by oath before the gods. Blessings and curses were listed for those who obeyed or disobeyed the covenant. Thus a relationship was established between two kings.

Sometimes a vassal was particularly faithful to the great king. Then, perhaps, the great king would thank the vassal with a gift, such as a piece of land. So the great king would make a covenant or treaty giving the vassal this land. This is a *royal grant covenant*. It is a unilateral, unconditional promise. The gift is promised unconditionally to the vassal.

There were also *parity treaties*. This is a treaty between equals. Two kings of equal power could make a parity treaty.

It is interesting to notice that these three types of covenant are found in the Old Testament.

Parity treaties are between equals. For example, Abraham and Abimelech made a treaty or covenant (Gen 21:27), as did Isaac and Abimelech (Gen 26:28). Parity treaties existed between kings of similar power, such as King Hiram and King Solomon (1 Kgs 5:12), King Asa and King Benhadad (1 Kgs 15:19) and King Ahab and King Benhadad (1 Kgs 20:34).

But when God makes a covenant, there is no parity: God is the Great King; we are the vassals. The Bible contains two types of divine covenants: some of these covenants resemble the suzerain-vassal treaty while others are like the royal grant treaties.

The Noahic Covenant

The first biblical covenant is the one made with Noah and his family. After the flood, God promised never again to destroy the earth by a flood (Gen 9:8-11).

This covenant is like a royal grant treaty. It is a unilateral, unconditional promise. The Great King (God) makes an unconditional promise. It does not depend on human behavior. It is a gracious promise made to Noah, his vassal, and all of his descendants.

This covenant was sealed by "the sign of the covenant" (Gen 9:12,17). The sign of the covenant is the rainbow. The rainbow is God's oath that his promise will be upheld.

The Abrahamic Covenants

Abraham was elected by God for a special purpose. Two covenants formalized this relationship.

The first covenant is found in Genesis 15. There God promised Abram descendents and land. He sealed this promise with an amazing ritual.

It was evening. Abram was told to take three animals and cut them in half. He laid out the pieces of the animals and two birds. When Abram fell asleep, a smoking fire pot—representing God himself —passed between the parts of the animals. This action is a self-maledictory oath. Here God promised that if he would break his promise—and God never breaks his promise—he should become like the dead animals. With this solemn oath God promised Abram the land.[3]

---

[3] Another self-maledictory oath is found in Jeremiah 34. Some people in Jerusalem made a covenant oath to free their Jewish slaves. To seal the oath, they killed a calf and walked between the pieces. But when the people broke their covenant promise, God said that he would treat them like the calf they cut in two (see Jer 34:8-20, esp. vs. 18).

This covenant is a royal grant treaty. God, the Great King, promised his servant Abram the land. It was an unconditional, unilateral covenant. It was a gracious promise to Abram who had been faithful.

The second Abrahamic covenant is found in Genesis 17. There God made a covenant between himself and Abraham. It was a conditional, bilateral (two-sided) covenant. Each party had its obligations.

God promised to be Abraham's God. God said, "I will establish my covenant . . . to be your God" (Gen 17:7). God would bless Abraham and be his God.

Abraham's part was to keep the covenant. As a sign of their commitment to God, the males in Abraham's family were to be circumcised. This was "the sign of the covenant" (Gen 17:11). (The females were included in the covenant without any female circumcision because they were part of the family or household.)

With this covenant, God entered into a personal relationship with Abraham and his family. Those who kept the terms of the covenant were in a good relationship with God, but those who broke the covenant would be cut off (Gen. 17:14).

The Genesis story suggests that Isaac and Jacob, despite their short-comings, remained in the covenant. But Ishmael and Esau, even though they had the sign of the covenant on their flesh, put themselves outside of this special relationship with God through their unbelief and disobedience.

The Sinaitic Covenant

In a sense, the Sinaitic covenant is a continuation of the Abrahamic covenants. In Genesis, God entered into a relationship with Abraham and his family; in Exodus, God entered into a relationship with the people of Israel.

The Sinaitic covenant was established at Mount Sinai. There God revealed the terms of the covenant. We have these terms especially in Exodus 20.

God first of all reminded Israel of his electing grace to his people: "I am Yahweh your God, who brought you out of Egypt, out of the land of slavery" (Ex 20:2). Already a relationship existed. Already God had shown his love to Israel.

The main requirement was for Israel to be faithful to God: "You shall have no other gods before me" (Ex 20:3). This is the same requirement that is in a marriage relationship. A husband and wife must be faithful to each other: don't get entangled with another woman or man!

After that, the other commands follow. We find the basic commands in Exodus 20 and the other laws in the next three chapters. The Book of the Covenant is the laws found from Exodus 20:23 to 23:19.

Then the people agreed to the terms of the covenant. After they heard the words of God, they promised: "Everything Yahweh has said we will do" (Ex 24:3).

Then Moses ratified the covenant with the blood of bulls. The bulls were killed and the blood was collected and sprinkled both on the altar and on the people. This represented God's oath and the people's oath. Moses called it "the blood of the covenant" (Ex 24:8).

Then Moses and the leaders of Israel climbed the mountain and ate and drank with God. They had communion with God. This fellowship meal is a picture of the Lord's Supper that we celebrate today.

Jeremiah tells us that God married Israel at Mount Sinai. God said, "I remember the devotion of your youth, how as a bride you loved me and followed me through the desert" (Jer 2:2).

Covenant Renewals

As time passed and new generations arose, this Sinaitic covenant was renewed.

Forty years after the covenant at Mount Sinai, the Israelites were on the plains of Moab ready to enter the Promised Land. There Moses renewed the covenant with Israel. The laws of Deuteronomy were:

> The terms of the covenant which Yahweh commanded Moses
> to make with the Israelites in Moab, in addition to the covenant
> he had made with them at Horeb.
>
> —Deut 29:1

Some years later, Joshua renewed the covenant with Israel at Shechem (Josh 24:25). The people renewed their vows to serve Yahweh only, and they were reminded of the Mosaic laws.

During the reign of King Josiah, the neglected Book of the Law was found in the temple. The king read the Book of the Covenant to the people, and both the king and the people made a covenant before God (2 Kgs 23:1-3).

After the exile, Ezra gathered the people in Jerusalem and read the Law. The people then confessed their sins and bound "themselves with a curse and an oath to follow the Law of God given through Moses" (Neh 10:29). This was another covenant renewal ceremony.

Since the Sinaitic covenant was conditional, it was imperative that every generation renew their commitment to God through the covenant.

The Davidic Covenant

In his grace, God also made an unconditional covenant with David. God promised David that "your house and your kingdom will endure forever before me; your throne will be established forever" (2 Sam 7:16).

This is an unconditional promise. It is like a royal grant treaty. The Great King made an unconditional promise to David that his royal line would last forever.

But during the exile, it seemed that God had broken his promise. The author of Psalm 89 remembered God's words to David. God had said, "I have made a covenant with my chosen one, I have sworn to David my servant, 'I will establish your line forever'" (Ps 89:3-4).

But now the Jews were in Babylon. Had God broken his promise? The psalmist wondered whether God had "renounced the covenant with [his] servant" (Ps 89:39). But the Davidic covenant was fulfilled in Jesus Christ. Many years later, the angel Gabriel told Mary that her son would "reign over the house of Jacob forever; his kingdom [would] never end" (Lk 1:32-33).

The New Covenant

The Jews were in Babylonian captivity because they had repeatedly broken the Sinaitic covenant. Continual idolatry was the same as spiritual adultery.

In the book of Jeremiah, God said that "they broke my covenant though I was a husband to them" (Jer 31:32). So in his grace God decided to make a new covenant. God said,

> The time is coming . . . when I will make a new covenant with
> the house of Israel and with the house of Judah. . . . I will put

my law in their minds and write it on their hearts. *I will be their God, and they will be my people.*

—Jer 31:31,33

These words in italics summarize the essence of the biblical covenants of grace.

The book of Hebrews tells us that this new covenant was fulfilled in Christ (see Hebrews 8). The blood of Jesus is the "blood of the covenant, which is poured out for many for the forgiveness of sins" (Mt 26:28). The death of Jesus is the ground of the new covenant.

The Holy Spirit is the facilitator of the new covenant. It is he who would write God's law on our hearts (Jer 31:33; Ezek 36:26-27).

The new covenant is a conditional covenant. It depends on our faith in Jesus. If we believe in Jesus, then God will be our God, and we will be his people. But if we do not believe, then we are not part of this covenant relationship.

The purpose of the Abrahamic, Sinaitic and new covenants is to establish a relationship between God and his people. God desires that everyone be in a good relationship with him.

Study Questions

1. What is the definition of covenant?
2. What is the difference between a suzerain-vassal covenant and a royal grant covenant?
3. What is the summary of the covenant that God made with Abraham in Genesis 17?
4. What is the essence of the covenant that God made with Israel at Mount Sinai?
5. Did God break his covenant with David, as Psalm 89 asks?
6. What is the ground of the new covenant?
7. Describe how we can be part of the new covenant.

CHAPTER 10

LAW AND HOLINESS

At Mount Sinai, God entered into a covenant relationship with Israel. This relationship was summarized in the words: "I am your God, and you are my people." Israel was in a special and exclusive relationship with God.

But the world that Israel lived in was a hostile and evil world. It was sinful and pagan. Israel was to be a holy nation in this evil world. God called Israel "a kingdom of priests and a holy nation" (Ex 19:6).

In the world there were two realms of existence: a realm of holiness and cleanness, and a realm of sin and uncleanness. A priest should be able to "distinguish between the holy and the profane, and the unclean and the clean" (Lev 10:10).

The profane or common (*hol*) is the opposite of the holy (*qadosh*); the unclean (*tame*) is the opposite of the clean (*tahor*).

> The Old Testament occasionally treats uncleanness and sin as more or less identical. . . . There is, so to speak, a sphere of evil and death that continually threatens man's life: it is called uncleanness [and] sin . . .[1]

---

[1] See H. Ringren, "Tame," in *Theological Dictionary of the Old Testament* 5:332; C. Rodd, *Glimpses of a Strange Land*, p. 10.

The Torah or law was given in this context. It was given to the holy nation of Israel in the context of a sinful and unclean world. The purpose of the law was to create and maintain a sphere of holiness and cleanness.

Traditionally we have understood the law as being command and obligation. But the Torah is also grace. The Torah both creates holiness and demands holiness.

The Law Creates Holiness And Cleanness

The Torah is a means of grace. The law is a means whereby holiness and cleanness are brought to Israel. One author speaks of the "sacramental dimension" of the Torah.[2] The law—like our sacraments—was a means of grace.

The book of Exodus has detailed prescriptions for the building of the tabernacle and the ark of the covenant. This was necessary because God was going to dwell there. God said, "Have them make a sanctuary for me, and I will dwell among them" (Ex 25:8). Later God said, "I will dwell among the Israelites and be their God" (Ex 29:45).

When the tabernacle was finished, "the glory of Yahweh filled the tabernacle" (Ex 40:34). God was with them. This was grace.

The ark of the covenant was the particular place where God would meet his people. God said, "There, above the cover between the two cherubim that are over the ark of the Testimony, I will meet with you" (Ex 25:22).

The Torah offers the presence of the holy God to Israel. This is rich grace indeed.

The sacrificial system of the Torah was also a means of grace. The sacrifices and Levitical rituals offered Israel holiness and cleanness.

---

[2]W. Brueggemann, *Theology of the Old Testament*, p. 582.

The sin offerings and guilt offerings offered forgiveness of sins and holiness. Through these sacrifices the priest made atonement for sin, and the person was forgiven (e.g., Lev 4:26,31,35).

The Day of Atonement was a special time when cleanness or holiness was obtained. Atonement was made for the holy place, the Tent of Meeting, the altar, the priests and all the people of the community (Lev 16:33). On that day, atonement was made for the people to cleanse them. Then they were clean from all their sins (Lev 16:30).

Cleanness from diseases and impurities was also obtained through the priestly system. A woman who gave birth should make atonement and be clean (Lev 12:7). A person who was cured from an infectious disease must go to the priest to be proclaimed clean. The priest then would "sacrifice the sin offering and make atonement for the one to be cleansed from his uncleanness" (Lev 14:19).

A priest would also purify a house that was cleansed from mildew. He would sacrifice a bird and "make atonement for the house, and it will be clean" (Lev 14:53). Atonement was also made for male or female bodily discharges (Lev 15:15,30).

Holiness comes from both God and from the response of the people. The Torah said: "Sanctify yourselves and be holy because I am Yahweh your God. . . . I am Yahweh who makes you holy" (Lev 20:7-8).

The Law Demands Ritual Holiness and Cleanness

As a holy people, Israel were to live a life separate from the nations. God said to Israel:

> You are to be holy to me because I, Yahweh, am holy, and I
> have set you apart from the nations to be my own.
>
> —Lev 20:26

Therefore they were to "make a distinction between clean and unclean animals and between unclean and clean birds" (Lev 20:25).

As a holy people the Israelites were not to eat any unclean animals. God said:

> Sanctify yourselves and be holy, because I am holy. Do not make yourselves unclean by any creature that moves about on the ground. . . . Be holy because I am holy.
>
> —Lev 11:44-45

The tabernacle was holy and off limits for the people. Only Aaron and his sons could serve there. "Anyone else who comes near the sanctuary must be put to death" (Num 18:7).

The ark of the covenant and other furniture were holy. Even the Levites must not go near the furnishings of the sanctuary or the altar or they would die (Num 18:3).

The priests were holy to God. The people should regard them as holy because they offered up holy food. God said: "Consider them holy, because I, Yahweh, who makes you holy, am holy" (Lev 21:6-8).

God's name was holy. God said: "Do not profane my holy name. I must be acknowledged as holy by the Israelites" (Lev 22:32).

The Sabbath day was holy. After the six days of creation, God "blessed the Sabbath day and made it holy." Therefore the Israelites were to remember the Sabbath day and keep it holy (Ex 20:8-11).

Other feasts were also holy feasts. Leviticus lists these feasts and calls them "holy assemblies" (Lev 23:1). During these feasts, no regular work was to be done. They were set aside in Israel's calendar.

The Torah demanded that God's people be holy and clean. God's people were to be separate from the nations. Many of the rituals in the Torah symbolized this distinctive identity. These rituals symbolized Israel's holiness and cleanness before God.

The Law Demands Ethical Holiness And Cleanness

God's people were to be holy in all of their life. The Torah demands holiness in the people's relationship to God and to their neighbor.

The Decalogue or Ten Commandments governs these relationships. The first four commands relate to our relationship with God; the next six commands deal with our relations to our neighbor.

The primary command is the first one: "You shall have no other gods before me" (Ex 20:3). At Mount Sinai, Israel entered into a covenantal relationship with God. The first command defines this relationship. Israel was in covenant with Yahweh; she was married to God; so they should not be in a relationship with any other god.

Idolatry is a form of pollution or uncleanness. This is particularly clear in the prophets. Jeremiah asks Israel: "How can you say that you are not unclean, that you have not gone after the Baals?" (Jer 2:23). "Woe to you Jerusalem! How long will it be before you are made clean?" (Jer 13:27).

Ezekiel accuses Jerusalem of becoming unclean through her idols (Ezek 22:4). Judah made the land unclean with their idols (Ezek 36:18).

The Holiness Code (Lev 17-26) forbids pagan religious practices which defile (*halal*) God's name. The sacrifice of children to Molech defiles the name of God (Lev 18:21). God's people were not to practice divination or sorcery (Lev 19:26). Consulting mediums and spiritists defiles God's people (Lev 19:31).

Swearing falsely by God's name defiles his name (Lev 19:12). God's Sabbath is holy; defiling the Sabbath is punishable by death (Ex 31:14).

Holiness and cleanness is also expected in an Israelite's relations with his or her neighbors. The last six of the Ten Commandments regulate the person's relations with his or her neighbors.

Leviticus 19 opens with the words: "Be holy because I, Yahweh your God, am holy" (Lev 19:2). In this chapter, holiness relates to all of life. There are commands relating to proper worship of God. There are also laws about our relations to our neighbor.

On the social level, one must honor one's father and mother. One should not steal or lie or deceive another person. Sexual purity is commanded. Respect should be given to the elderly. Honesty must be practiced in the marketplace. Justice must be practiced in the courts.

This chapter has a remarkable concern for the poor and needy. In harvesting one's crop, it is important to think of the poor and the alien (Lev 19:10). The alien should not be mistreated; instead, the alien should be loved (Lev 19:33-34). The basic principle of love for one's neighbor is stated (Lev 19:18).

Failure to live a holy life makes a person unclean. Israel became unclean through their sinful deeds (Ps 106:39). Judah was unclean because of her sins (Mic 2:10).

The demand for holiness or cleanness even extended to cleanliness in the camp. The people were not to relieve themselves anywhere; instead, they were to make latrines for "your camp must be holy" (Deut 23:14).

But the temptation to be like the nations was strong. Once Israel desired a king "like all the nations" (1 Sam 8:5,20). But God was not happy with their request. Israel had again forgotten her distinctive calling to be holy.

The Christian and the Law

Not all of the Old Testament laws are directly relevant to the New Testament Christian. Often the present-day believer must look for the ethical or spiritual principle behind such laws.

Civil laws were legal codes for the nation of Israel. Often they had specific penalties for a sin. For example: "Anyone who curses his father or mother must be put to death" (Ex 21:17). The ethical principle is clear: do not curse your parents. But the legal penalty will not apply literally to the Christian today.

Moral laws have more general relevance. For example: "Do not steal. Do not lie. Do not deceive one another" (Lev 19:11). These are moral laws with universal relevance.

Ceremonial laws are fulfilled in Jesus Christ who is our high priest and atoning sacrifice. We do not offer sacrifices specified in Leviticus. Rather you should "offer your bodies as living sacrifices, holy and pleasing to God" (Rom 12:1).

The laws about cleanness are also fulfilled with the coming of Jesus. When Peter saw a vision of unclean animals, he was told to kill and eat (Acts 10). The ceremonial laws are no longer literally applicable to the believer.

The church is holy because it is redeemed by the blood of Jesus. This church is now called to be holy and clean in this world. We are to be in the world but not of the world.

Study Questions

1. How did the Torah create cleanness in Israel?
2. How was the Torah a means of grace for Israel?
3. What was the purpose of the law in the Old Testament?
4. What kinds of ritual holiness did the law demand in Deut 14:1-21?
5. List five ethical principles in the Ten Commandments.
6. What are some social principles that we can derive from Leviticus 19?
7. What are some social principles found in Deuteronomy 24?

CHAPTER 11

SALVATION

The Old Testament proclaims that salvation comes from God. When the Israelites came through the waters of the Red Sea, they testified that Yahweh had become their salvation (Ex 15:2). When Jonah was rescued by the great fish, he affirmed that "salvation comes from Yahweh" (Jon 2:9). The psalmist says that God "alone is my rock and my salvation" (Ps 62:2,6).

God is often called the Savior or Redeemer of Israel. The psalmist calls him "my rock and my Redeemer" (Ps 19:14). The book of Isaiah commonly speaks of God as Israel's Redeemer (e.g., Is 41:14; 43:14).

Often salvation is physical deliverance. When Israel was trapped by the Egyptian army, Yahweh "saved [them] from the hand of the Egyptians" (Ex 14:30).

Jonah's salvation was primarily physical, although it led him to some spiritual reflection (Jon 2:1-9). Likewise, the judges "saved" Israel (e.g., Judg 3:9,31). This salvation was physical, although it was preceded by repentance.

The psalmist was frequently threatened by external enemies. He would then cry out for God to save him (e.g., Ps 7:1). After this deliverance, he would thank God for this salvation.

God was Israel's Savior and Redeemer. He saves from sickness and difficult situations. He delivers the king from military defeat. He provides physical salvation to those who trust in him. But what of salvation from sin? How is the Old Testament person saved from sin?

Atonement

Sin is rebellion against God. Sin is a serious offence against God. It is necessary that sin be covered or removed for a person to be saved.

In his grace the holy God provided the possibility of atonement or covering of sins. The Hebrew word for "to atone" is *kipper*. This word may originally have meant to cover sins, but its main meaning is to expiate or to atone for sin.

The Levitical laws made provisions for atonement through the offering of sacrifices. If the community or a member of the community sins unintentionally, a sin offering or guilt offering must be made. An animal would be sacrificed: "in this way the priest will make atonement for them, and they will be forgiven" (e.g., Lev 4:20,26,31).

Once a year, atonement was made for the sins of all the people. This was the great Day of Atonement. Then a bull would be sacrificed as atonement for the priest and his family. One goat would be sacrificed to make atonement for the people's sins. Another goat sent into the desert would symbolically carry the people's sins and thus make atonement for them. Thus, "atonement is to be made once a year for all the sins of the Israelites" (Lev 16:34).

The animal sacrifices were a picture of the gravity of sin and the fact that a price had to be paid for our sins. These sacrifices also pointed to the sacrifice of the Lamb of God on the cross of Calvary.

But sacrifices without a contrite heart were meaningless. God said to sinful Israel, "Even though you bring me burnt offerings and grain offerings, I will not accept them" (Amos 5:22). David reminds us that "the sacrifices of God are a broken spirit; a broken and contrite heart, O God, you will not despise" (Ps 51:17).

Thus we discover that atonement was sometimes made without sacrifice. When the people sinned with the golden calf, Moses offered to "make atonement for [their] sin" (Ex 32:30). He did this through intercessory prayer.

At the beginning of Isaiah's ministry, a seraph took a burning coal and put it to Isaiah's lips saying, "Your guilt is taken away and your sin atoned for" (Is 6:7).

In the end, atonement occurs through God's grace. At a difficult period in Israel's history, it was God who atoned for sins. The psalmist prayed, "When we were overwhelmed by sins, you atoned for our transgressions" (Ps 65:3). This, of course, was without sacrifice. This atonement was of God's grace.

Forgiveness of Sins

Forgiveness of sins is often the result of atonement. "Atonement" and "forgiveness" are frequently linked together in Leviticus. When the priest offers a sin offering or guilt offering, he makes "atonement" and the person is "forgiven" (e.g., Lev 4:20; 5:16,18). This is the important ritual of sacrifice and forgiveness.

But ultimately forgiveness was dependent on Israel's confession of sin and God's forgiving grace. Solomon prayed that if the people sin and then turn and confess their sins, God should "hear from heaven and forgive the sin" (1 Kgs 8:33-34). God responded to Solomon that:

> If my people, who are called by my name, will humble themselves and pray . . . I will hear from heaven and will forgive their sin.
>
> —2 Chr 7:14

After his sin with Bathsheba, David prayed that God would have mercy and blot out his transgressions and cleanse him from his sin (Ps 51:1-2).

The psalmist elsewhere cries for mercy because with God "there is forgiveness" (Ps 130:4). God is the one who "forgives all my sins and heals all my diseases" (Ps 103:3).

Salvation and forgiveness of sins are ultimately a matter of human confession and divine grace.

Fearing and Loving God

So how was the Old Testament person saved? What did he or she have to do to be saved? Was the Old Testament person saved by faith or by works?

A believer in the Old Testament is one who fears, loves, trusts and obeys God. A believer is one who stands in a good and trusting relationship with God.

Often the believer is described as one who *fears* God. Originally, fear had the idea of being afraid of someone or something. When God spoke to Moses from the burning bush, Moses feared or was afraid to look at God (Ex 3:6). When God pronounced judgment, "the earth feared and was quiet" (Ps 76:8).

But the fear of God eventually came to mean the reverence or worship of God. The Israelite midwives were those who "feared God" and did the right thing (Ex 1:17,21). When God delivered Israel from Egypt, the people "feared Yahweh and they believed in Yahweh and in Moses his servant" (Ex 14:31).

Jonah claimed to be one who "fears" or believes in Yahweh (Jon 1:9). After the sea became quiet, the sailors "greatly feared Yahweh and offered a sacrifice to Yahweh" (Jon 1:16).

The book of Deuteronomy repeatedly commands the Israelites to fear Yahweh and serve him (Deut 6:13). The fear of God, then, is a deep trust in God.

In Deuteronomy, the *love* of God is linked closely with the fear of God. The law commands the people to fear God, walk in his ways, love him, serve him and obey him (Deut 10:12).

The summary of the Torah is the command to "love Yahweh your God" with all of one's heart, soul and strength (Deut 6:5). This is the primary command.

Although obedience to God is present in Deuteronomy, the fear and love of God are primary. The relationship with God is primary; the obedience to God and his law follows from this relationship.

The Old Testament person, then, was saved through being in a good relationship with God. The believer was saved when he or she loved and feared God.

The fear and love of God are parallel to the New Testament justification by faith. Just as faith in the New Testament brings a person into a relationship with God, so the fear and love of God bring a person into a similar relationship in the Old Testament.

In a few significant passages, the Old Testament speaks of having *faith* and trust in God. The classic example of faith is Abraham. When God promised the aged Abram offspring like the stars, "Abram believed Yahweh" (Gen 15:6). Abram's faith was tested on Mount Moriah. At the end of the test, the angel concluded that Abram feared God (Gen 22:12).

After the exodus, the people "feared Yahweh and they believed in Yahweh and in Moses his servant" (Ex 14:31). The fear of God and faith in God are similar.

After Jonah's sermon, "the Ninevites believed God" and they were saved (Jon 3:5).

God's words to King Ahaz stressed the importance of faith: "If you do not believe, you will not stand at all" (Is 7:9). King Hezekiah, by contrast, trusted in God in a time of crisis (2 Kgs 18:5).

An Old Testament scholar concluded that "in the Old Testament . . . there already exists what Paul calls the justification of the sinner."[1]

Obedience to the law is important, but it is not a means of salvation. The book of Deuteronomy often calls upon the believer to keep and obey God's law. The law stipulates that those who obey and do the commands will be blessed; those who do not obey and do the commands will be cursed (Deut 28:1,15).

But these conditions are given to people already in a covenant relationship with God. These conditions also assume the primary command of loving and fearing God. Deuteronomy teaches a faith-obedience. The law expects that a person will "trust and obey," in that sequence. The trust comes first; the obedience comes second.

Covenant Membership

Salvation, then, is a matter of being in a good relationship with God. A righteous person is in a good relationship with God; a wicked person is not.

The covenant concept summarizes this relationship. The bilateral Abrahamic and Sinaitic covenants established a personal relationship between God and his people.

The summary of the covenant is: "I will be your God, and you will be my people" (Lev 26:12; cf. Jer 31:33). The covenant is a good relationship between God and his people.

One theologian said: "The fundamental redemptive idea in Israel . . . was the idea of its being in covenant with Yahweh. This

---

[1]H.D. Preuss, *Old Testament Theology*, 2:184.

embraced all."[2] Another writer said: "A person is righteous who has fulfilled the claims which derived from the covenantal relationship."[3]

The Abrahamic covenant in Genesis 17 and the Sinaitic covenant in Exodus are conditional covenants. A person who is faithful to God is part of the covenant relationship; a person who rejects God has put himself out of the covenant.

In the Abrahamic covenant, male circumcision was a condition of the covenant. "Any uncircumcised male . . . will be cut off from his people; he has broken my covenant" (Gen 17:14). (The females were included in the covenant through the male head of the household. The Bible does not condone female circumcision.)

Refusal to obey God's commands is a breaking of the covenant. The book of Leviticus says that those who refuse to carry out God's commands have violated the covenant and will be punished (Lev 26:14-17).

But the primary form of covenant-breaking was idolatry. The Sinaitic covenant binds Israel to Yahweh. But when Israel goes after other gods, then they are committing spiritual adultery. Then they are cut off from the covenant.

In Deuteronomy, God predicts that Israel "will turn to other gods and worship them, rejecting me and breaking my covenant" (Deut 31:20). Idolatry constitutes the breaking of the covenant. Idolatry brings God's punishment.

The prophet Hosea vividly portrays this fact. The prophet was to take an adulterous wife "because the land is guilty of the vilest adultery in departing from Yahweh" (Hos 1:2). Hosea's main point is that idolatry is spiritual adultery.

---

[2]A.B. Davidson, *The Theology of the Old Testament*, pp. 238-39.
[3]B. Childs, *Old Testament Theology in a Canonical Context*, p. 208.

In adultery, a person breaks the covenant with his or her spouse and goes off with another person. In idolatry, a person breaks the covenant with his God and goes off with another god. Both adultery and idolatry are a form of covenant-breaking.

The book of Kings tells the history of the Assyrian captivity of Israel. The question is asked: Why did this happen? The answer is clear: Israel broke the covenant with God. "When Yahweh made a covenant with the Israelites, he commanded them, 'Do not worship any other gods'" (2 Kgs 17:35). But because of their persistent idolatry, Israel was carried off into captivity. "This happened because they had not obeyed Yahweh their God, but had violated his covenant" (2 Kgs 18:12).

Salvation in the Old Testament is found by being in a good relationship with God. Salvation occurs when one fears and loves God. Salvation is present when one believes in God and tries to obey his commandments. Salvation occurs when a person is in a good covenant relationship with God through a trust and love of God.

Study Questions

1. How did sacrifices atone for sin?
2. What does God think about sacrifices that do not come from a contrite heart?
3. How did the Old Testament person receive forgiveness of sins?
4. What does it mean to fear God?
5. Is the Old Testament person justified by faith or by works?
6. What is the relationship between salvation and covenant?
7. How was the Old Testament person saved?

CHAPTER 12

WORSHIP

Worship is the response of the believer to God's grace. Worship is "encounter with God," a meeting with God.[1] It includes prayer, sacrifice and praise.

Worship can occur on a private, individual basis, at any place. But worship can also happen in public, with other believers, in a "sacred" place. Worship can be individual or corporate; it can be spontaneous or it can be liturgical.

The law prescribes forms of public worship. But worship was already happening from the beginning of salvation history.

Early Biblical Worship

In the beginning, God communed with the man and the woman. God walked in the Garden with Adam and Eve. Later, Enoch "walked with God" (Gen 5:24). This early communion was a form of worship.

When Abram arrived in Canaan, he "built an altar to Yahweh, who had appeared to him" (Gen 12:7). At Bethel, Abram "built an altar to Yahweh and called on the name of Yahweh" (Gen 12:8; cf. 13:4). This is early worship. God appeared to Abram, and Abram responded with offerings and with prayer.

---

[1] H.H. Rowley, *Worship in Ancient Israel*, p. 271.

When God appeared to Jacob on his way to Haran, Jacob responded by consecrating a stone pillar and making a vow (Gen 28:18-22). This was worship. Later, a unique worship event occurred when Jacob wrestled with God (Gen 32:22-30).

Personal, private worship continued during the time of the exodus. God appeared to Moses at the burning bush, and Moses removed his sandals and hid his face (Ex 3:5-6). At Mount Sinai, Moses and about 70 others went up the mountain where "they saw God, and they ate and drank" (Ex 24:9-11).

Before the battle of Jericho, God appeared to Joshua to encourage him, and Joshua removed his sandals because he was on holy ground (Josh 5:13-15).

Early worship, then, was usually a personal encounter with God. It occurred in private and public places.

During the period of the judges and the early monarchy, worship often took place at local shrines. There were shrines in Mizpah (1 Sam 7:9), Ramah (1 Sam 7:17), Gilgal (1 Sam 10:8), Bethel (1 Sam 7:16) and Shiloh (1 Sam 1-2). Most of these were places where Samuel offered sacrifices.[2]

A man named Elkanah once went to the shrine of Shiloh "to worship and sacrifice" to God (1 Sam 1:3). His wife, Hannah, came to pray. God spoke to her through the priest Eli. This is an example of worship at a local shrine.

The prophet Amos testifies to the continued function of some of these shrines in the eighth century (Amos 4:4; 5:4-5).

---

[2]H.H. Rowley, *Worship in Ancient Israel*, p. 63.

The Central Sanctuary

The Torah instructed the people to make a tabernacle which was a center of worship. At that sanctuary, God would "dwell among them" and he would "meet" them (Ex 25:8,22).

In time, the temple—the First Temple and the Second Temple— became the center of Israel's worship. (The First Temple was built by Solomon and destroyed by the Babylonians; the Second Temple was built by the returned exiles and destroyed by the Romans.)

The temple was a dwelling place of God. When the temple was completed, "the glory of Yahweh filled his temple" (1 Kgs 8:11).

The temple was a main center where the people could meet God. The psalmist wrote: "How lovely is your dwelling place, O Yahweh of hosts. I yearn, even faint for the courts of Yahweh" (Ps 84:1-2). Often the psalmist would come to the temple when in distress.

The temple was holy since it belonged to God. Certain conditions were necessary for entering the temple. The psalmist asks, "Yahweh, who may dwell in your sanctuary? Who may live on your holy hill?" Only those who keep God's commands may be in God's temple (Ps 15). Again, only the one "who has clean hands and a pure heart" may "stand in his holy place" (Ps 24:3-4).

The temple was the place of regular sacrifices and offerings where people praised God and confessed their sins. It was a place of instruction where the Torah was read. It was a place of prayer. But it was also a place of singing and dancing. The Old Testament gives significant examples of dancing as a form of worship (Ps 87:7; 149:3; 150:4).[3]

The temple was a center of celebration. There were three main festival seasons in the year: the Feast of Unleavened Bread and the

---

[3]H.H. Rowley, *Worship in Ancient Israel*, p. 140.

Passover; the Harvest Festival and the Feast of Firstfruits; and the Feast of Booths.

The Priest

The Torah made provisions for God's presence to be realized in Israel. The Torah was a means of grace for Israel. The priests were officials who facilitated this experience of God's presence and grace.

The priest was a mediator between God and the people. The priest stood between God and the people. The priest had "a twofold duty of teaching and intercession."[4] This twofold duty can be seen in the blessing of Moses, where the Levites were to teach the Torah to Israel and to offer incense and sacrifices to God (Deut 33:10). The priest represents God to the people; and the priest represents the people to God.

In the first place, the priest was to represent God to the people. He did this especially through the teaching of the law. The Torah said that the priests should read the law once every seven years to the people (Deut 31:10-11).

Jeremiah talks of the "teaching of the law by the priest" (Jer 18:18). Malachi says that the people should receive instruction from the priest, for "he is the messenger of Yahweh of hosts" (Mal 2:7).

Ezra, "the priest and scribe," once read the law to the people for a whole day. This led to the people's confession of their sins (Neh 8:1-9).

The priests were experts in the law. A priest should be able to distinguish between the clean and unclean as well as to teach the laws (Lev 10:10-11). At the time of the prophet Haggai, the priests were called on to declare what was clean and what was unclean (Hag 2:10-13).

---

[4]E. Jacob, *Theology of the Old Testament*, p. 247.

The priests also represented God to the people by giving God's blessing. In the book of Numbers, God told Aaron and his sons how to bless the Israelites. They should say, "May Yahweh bless you and keep you . . . and make his face shine upon you . . . and give you peace" (Num 6:24-26). The priest represented God to the people.

But the priest also represented the people to God. When the people sinned, the priest would offer sacrifices to atone for their sins. The priest was responsible for sacrificing the sin offering and the guilt offering to achieve atonement. Once a year, on the Day of Atonement, the priest would make atonement "for all the sins of the Israelites" (Lev 16:34).

Intercession was also part of the priest's duty. We know that Moses interceded to God for the people more than once (Ex 32:31; Num 14:13-19). The reference to Levi offering incense suggests priestly intercession (Deut 33:10).

The Israelite priesthood reminds us of Jesus Christ who was the great High Priest who made a sacrifice for our sins once for all and who continually intercedes as a priest for his people.

Sacrifices and Offerings

A central part of worship was the offering of sacrifices and offerings. Three types stand out. A sacrifice might be a gift to God, a form of communion or expiation.[5]

Some offerings were presented as a gift to God. The normal term for this sacrifice is *minḥah*. The purpose of this sacrifice could be "total self-surrender" to God, thanksgiving or a form of appeasement.[6]

---

[5] E. Jacob, *Theology of the Old Testament*, pp. 268-69; cf. W. Eichrodt, *Theology of the Old Testament*, 1:144-72.
[6] W. Eichrodt, *Theology of the Old Testament*, 1:145.

Cain and Abel offered such offerings to God (Gen 4:3-5), but the heart of the one was right and the other was not. When Abram arrived in the Promised Land, he built altars and made such sacrifices (Gen 12:7-8).

The first chapter of Leviticus describes the burnt offering (*'olah*); the second chapter describes the grain offering (*minhah*). Both of these could function as a gift offering to God in worship.

A second type was the fellowship or peace offering. We find this sacrifice in the third chapter of Leviticus. This sacrifice was a form of communion between God and man.

The third type of sacrifice was one of expiation of sin. Sin offerings and guilt offerings were prescribed for atonement for sin. (We find these sacrifices in Leviticus 4 and 5.) They were performed on a regular basis.

The greatest event of atonement in the Old Testament was the Day of Atonement (*yom kippur*). This is when "atonement is to be made once a year for all the sins of the Israelites" (Lev 16:34).

Sacrifices are rituals which express one's relation to God. We live in thanksgiving, communion and confession before God. Sacrifices are meaningful only when the heart is right.

Feast and Festivals

The law required that all the male Israelites appear before God three times every year (Ex 34:23). The occasion was the three seasons of feasts in the calendar.[7] Obviously this was a time of celebration for the Israelites.

The first great time of celebration was the Feasts of Passover and Unleavened Bread. In the month of Abib, in March and April, the Israelites celebrated their exodus out of Egypt. During these festivals,

---

[7]See the charts in the *NIV Study Bible* by Exodus 12 and Leviticus 23.

they ate the Passover lamb and unleavened bread (cf. Lev 23:4-8). This was also the time of the barley harvest, at which time the Feast of Firstfruits was held (cf. Lev 23:9-14).

The second time of celebration was the Feast of Weeks or Harvest (cf. Lev 23:15-21; Ex 23:16a). This was an agricultural festival at the beginning of the wheat harvest. It was called the Feast of Weeks or Pentecost because it was 7 weeks or 50 days after the Feast of Unleavened Bread. This was held in the third month, in our May and June.

The third festival time was in the seventh month, in September and October, during the harvest of the orchards and vines. On the first day, the Feast of Trumpets was held; the Day of Atonement was on the tenth day; and the Feast of Tabernacles, Booths or Ingathering was held from the 15th to 21st of the month (cf. Lev 23:23-43).

In addition, on every seventh day the people were required to observe the Sabbath day (cf. Lev 23:3). The Sabbath day was a weekly day devoted to rest and fellowship with God. The Sabbath reminds us "that no business, however pressing, must be allowed to keep people from regularly seeking his fellowship." Also, "the joyful character of the day of rest also brings home to the worshiper that his God is a kindly Master."[8]

In the Genesis account, the Sabbath rest is compared to God's rest after the work of creation (Gen 2:2-3). This fact shows that the Sabbath was a source of blessing and "bears witness to the enthusiasm with which the pious Israelite rejoiced in this day of rest as an act of devotion."[9]

---

[8]W. Eichrodt, *Theology of the Old Testament*, 1:133.
[9]W. Eichrodt, *Theology of the Old Testament*, 1:133.

Psalms

The book of Psalms is the prayer book of Israel. It contains songs and prayers of Israel. There are four main types of psalms: hymns of praise, individual psalms of lament, communal psalms of lament, and songs of thanksgiving.

Hymns of praise were part of the temple liturgy. Psalm 100 is an example of a hymn of praise. "Shout for joy to Yahweh, all the earth. . . . Enter his gates with thanksgiving and his courts with praise" (Ps 100:1,4).

Psalm 98 is another hymn of praise. It calls on the people to sing a new song to God. It calls for the music of the harp, the human voice and the loud trumpet. Psalm 150 lists additional instruments. It was good to sing songs of praise in God's temple.

But sometimes disaster struck the nation. Then communal psalms of lament were sung. Psalms 79 and 80 cry to God after a national disaster: "How long, O Yahweh? Will you be angry forever?" (Ps 79:5). "Restore us, O God; make your face shine upon us that we may be saved" (Ps 80:3).

Psalm 137 is another communal psalm of lament. "By the rivers of Babylon we sat and wept" (Ps 137:1). This psalm was written in exile after the temple was destroyed. Perhaps it was sung or prayed in the synagogue.

Sometimes disaster struck an individual person. At times this person was the king. Then the person might write an individual psalm of lament. "O Yahweh, how many are my foes! How many rise up against me! . . . Arise, O Yahweh! Deliver me, O my God!" (Ps 3:1,7).

More than one third of the psalms are individual psalms of lament. Some of these psalms were first prayed at home. But later they were brought into the temple or the synagogue.

When God answered a prayer of lament, the people would thank God. They would write a hymn of thanksgiving. Psalm 116 is such a psalm. The psalmist writes,

> I love Yahweh, for he heard my voice . . . . The cords of death entangled me . . . . Then I called on the name of Yahweh . . . . When I was in great need, he saved me.
>
> —Ps 116:1-6

Psalm 118 is another psalm of thanksgiving. The psalmist praises God because "he answered by setting me free" (Ps 118:5). But this psalm is also a liturgical psalm. A procession is approaching the temple. The leader, probably the king, proclaims, "Open for me the gates of righteousness; I will enter and give thanks to Yahweh" (Ps 118:19).

Liturgical psalms are another category of psalms. Psalm 24 may also be a liturgical psalm. Possibly the ark of the covenant was being brought into the temple in procession. The leader proclaims, "Lift up your heads, O you gates; be lifted up, you ancient doors, that the King of glory may come in" (Ps 24:7). A liturgical drama follows. Someone asks, "Who is this King of glory?" The response is, "Yahweh strong and mighty, Yahweh mighty in battle" (Ps 24:8,10).

Other categories of psalms include royal psalms and pilgrimage psalms. The temple was a center of celebration and worship, and the Psalms assisted Israel in their worship.

Prayer

Prayer is at the heart of worship. Prayer is a personal encounter with God. Prayer can be done publicly in the temple or privately at one's home.

> Prayer, and indeed all true worship, is fundamentally communion with God. The greatest gift of God is himself, and

the supreme end of worship is to be lifted into the spirit of God,
to share his life, his thought, his purpose.
—H.H. Rowley, *Worship in Ancient Israel*, p. 264.

Many psalms express this communion. "I yearn, even faint for the courts of Yahweh; my heart and my flesh cry out for the living God" (Ps 84:2). "As the deer pants for streams of water, so I pant for you, O God" (Ps 42:1).

Study Questions

1. What is worship?
2. Give some examples of early worship in the Old Testament.
3. What are the two main functions of a priest?
4. What are the three basic types of sacrifice?
5. What are the three main times of festivals?
6. What are an individual psalm of lament and a communal psalm of lament?
7. What types of psalms are Psalm 13, 117, 129 and 137?

CHAPTER 13

WISDOM

How does a person know how to live? There are two ways. One can read the Scriptures, including the Torah, to understand God's will for our lives. But one can also consult local wisdom. So how do these two sources of ethics relate to each other?

Traditional Wisdom

Every culture has local wisdom. This wisdom is preserved in parables, proverbs and stories, often oral but sometimes written. This wisdom is often transmitted in the village around the fire in the evening.

The African culture has wisdom in a large number of proverbs: "When elephants fight, the grass suffers." "Sticks in a bundle are unbreakable." "One leg does not dance alone." "Silence is an answer."[1]

This local wisdom teaches a person how to live in this world. A person is taught the values of hard work, speaking the truth, respecting one's elders and a gentle answer. This local wisdom warns a person about potential dangers: laziness, rudeness, deceit and contentiousness. This wisdom is practical wisdom, teaching people how to live successfully in a sometimes difficult environment.

---

[1]See J. Crenshaw, *Old Testament Wisdom*, p. 4.

This wisdom comes from experience. Everyone can see that the farm of a lazy person produces nothing. Everyone knows that a hot-headed person gets into trouble. Everyone notes how a proud man falls and suffers embarrassment.

Over time, the wisdom gotten from experience is put into proverbs or stories. This becomes part of our culture.

This wisdom, then, is creational wisdom. It does not come from the Bible; instead, it comes from our experience in God's world. Every culture has this kind of wisdom.

Israel's Wisdom

Wisdom literature in the Old Testament is unique in that it contains only a few references to the salvation history of Israel. There are virtually no references to Abraham, Isaac, Jacob, Saul, David or the prophets. There are few allusions to Israel's election, covenants, priests and temple worship. Wisdom comes from creational or everyday life.

Probably Israel's wisdom originally developed in the towns and villages. Often it took the form of proverbs. We can find some of these in the book of Proverbs. "Lazy hands make a man poor." "He who gathers crops in summer is a wise son." "Hatred stirs up dissension." "He who heeds discipline shows the way to life." "He who holds his tongue is wise" (Prov 10:4,5,12,17,19).

Such wisdom is obvious and practical. A Christian, Muslim and traditionalist all know that laziness makes a man poor. We all know that hatred stirs up dissension. We know that it is prudent to hold our tongue. Such wisdom is common knowledge.

In the course of time, this wisdom was collected and brought to the royal court in Jerusalem. In the king's court, there were wise men and scribes. The book of Jeremiah suggests a separate class of wise men or sages in Israel (Jer 18:18).

Hushai is an example of a wise man attached to the court of David. Hushai's wisdom was successful in confusing Absalom in his coup attempt against his father David (2 Sam 17:5-16).

The book of Samuel tells about two wise women. A wise woman from Tekoa once gave King David advice in a time of crisis; another wise woman gave advice to a military commander (2 Sam 14:1-21; 20:16-22).

King Solomon is associated with wisdom. Wisdom flourished at his court. Probably there was a class of wise men and scribes in his royal court who collected and wrote down some of the local wisdom. Much of this wisdom is preserved for us in the book of Proverbs.

But this process continued after Solomon. We read in the book of Proverbs that men in the court of King Hezekiah continued the collection of such wisdom (Prov 25:1).

Wisdom and Law

It is clear that both wisdom and the law tell a person how to live. But while the law is part of God's special revelation, "wisdom theology is creation theology."[2]

In wisdom literature, there are two classes of people: the wise and the foolish. The wise will generally be successful; the foolish will usually fail. This is a natural law of creation.

In the law, there are two classes of people: the righteous and the wicked. The righteous are those who obey God's law; the wicked neglect the law. The righteous will be blessed; the wicked will be punished (see Deut 28:1-19). This is the moral order of the Torah.

At some point in time these two ethical systems were brought together. In the book of Proverbs and elsewhere, we observe that the wise people are the righteous ones; and the foolish people are the

---

[2]W. Zimmerli, quoted in R. Murphy, *The Tree of Life*, p. 118.

wicked ones. This is an indication that wisdom was brought into the temple or the synagogue.

One writer compares wisdom and Law to "two great streams" which flow together.[3] This happened when wisdom was brought into the temple or the synagogue. Later wisdom literature affirms that "the fear of Yahweh" is wisdom and the beginning of knowledge (Job 28:28; Prov 1:7).

Since Yahweh is both the creator of the world and the source of Israel's law, it is Yahweh who guarantees and upholds both the natural and moral world order. A wise and righteous person is bound to succeed; a foolish and wicked person is bound to fail.

A World-And-Life View

Wisdom tells one how to live well and succeed in this world. Wisdom is not an academic type of knowledge. It is practical knowledge. It is the ability of doing the right thing in a given situation.

Wisdom "is the intensely practical art of being skillful and successful in life. . . . Wisdom is religion outside of church."[4] Wisdom gives guidance in many areas in life.[5] It is a world-and-life view.

Wisdom teaches a family how to live. Parents should train their children in the fear of Yahweh. Children should listen to the instruction of the parents. A husband should be faithful to the wife. Adultery is a trap that leads to death. The wife should be industrious and hard-working.

Wisdom teaches people how to live together. We should be gentle towards one another. A hot temper destroys relationships. Gossip destroys friendships.

------

[3]J. Blenkinsopp, *Wisdom and Law in the Old Testament*, p. 17.
[4]W. Dyrness, *Themes in Old Testament Theology*, p. 189.
[5]See R.E. Clements, *Wisdom in Theology*, chs. 3-5.

Wisdom teaches basic economic values. Hard work will pay off. Laziness will ruin a person. Honesty in the marketplace is valued. False weights and balances are wrong.

Wisdom also teaches basic political values. A king should practice justice and righteousness. When a king does not rule justly, the people will suffer.

Wisdom like the Torah is a world-and-life view. Israel's religion impacts all of life. All of life belongs to God the Creator.

When the Wise Suffer

We have seen that both wisdom and the law presuppose a moral world order. They presuppose that the wise and righteous person will be successful and blessed, and the foolish and wicked person will fail and be cursed.

This is the law of retribution. One will be successful or unsuccessful depending on his actions. This rule is usually true.

But there are exceptions. Sometimes the righteous or wise person suffers; sometimes the foolish or the wicked person prospers. Why does this happen?

The book of Job wrestles with this question. Job was both a righteous and a wise person. Yet Job suffered. The book of Job asks why this happens.

There is no easy answer to this question. But in the end we confess that God is ultimately in control. God's wisdom transcends our own wisdom. God controls and directs history in directions that we may not understand. It takes faith to accept God's sovereignty in history and in our lives.

The book of Ecclesiastes was written in a difficult time in Israel's history. The Preacher exclaimed, "Vanity of vanities, all is vanity" or meaningless (Eccl 1:2). Life was meaningless partly because of the social oppression that was happening in the Preacher's time: "I saw the tears of the oppressed—and they have no comforter; power was on the side of their oppressors" (Eccl 4:1).

But life is also empty if it is lived apart from God. If one's life consists only of chasing after riches, then life will certainly be empty.

The wisdom preacher concludes: "Fear God and keep his commandments, for this is the whole duty of man" (Eccl 12:13). Success in life depends on living in harmony with God and our neighbor. This is true wisdom.

Study Questions

1. How is the wisdom in Proverbs creational wisdom?
2. What are the two classes of people in the Torah? What are the two classes of people in wisdom literature?
3. What will happen to the wise and the righteous? What will happen to the foolish and the wicked?
4. How is Old Testament wisdom a world-and-life view?
5. According to Ecclesiastes, why do righteous or wise people sometimes suffer?
6. According to Job, why do the righteous suffer?

CHAPTER 14

KINGSHIP IN ISRAEL

Ancient Israel had both a political and spiritual leadership. In the monarchy, the king was the political leader, and the priests and prophets were the spiritual leaders.

Yahweh is King

In the early days of her existence, Israel was a theocracy. (The word "theocracy" means a rule by God.) Israel did not have an earthly king: instead, God was her king. In this, Israel was unique among the nations.

When Israel came out of Egypt, she proclaimed that "Yahweh will reign" (Ex 15:18). God first ruled his people through Moses and Joshua. After Joshua God raised up judges to govern the people from time to time.

The Israelites once asked one of the judges to rule over them. But Gideon refused, saying, "Yahweh will rule over you" (Judg 8:23). When a son of Gideon wanted to become a king, another son told a parable mocking this idea (Judg 9:7-15).

Later the people asked the prophet Samuel for a king. But God responded by saying that with this request the people were rejecting God as king (1 Sam 8:7).

Samuel then warned the people that a king would exploit and oppress the people. A king would take their sons and daughters and the best part of the crops and flocks as his own. The king would "take a tenth of your flocks, and you yourselves will become his slaves" (1 Sam 8:17).

Rulers then and now tend to exploit the common people. Human rulers always seem to be chasing after money and power.

Israel's Monarchy

When Israel did receive a king, this kingship was not to be absolute. The king was under the rule of God. This was different from the nations. "Elsewhere the king was a god; in Israel it was God who was king."[1]

The book of Deuteronomy describes the ideal king. The king must not accumulate great wealth or many wives. The king must make a copy of the law and have it with him at all times. He must read the law so that he might fear God and obey the commands of the law (Deut 17:14-20). This remarkable passage tells us that the king of Israel was not above the law but was subject to it.

Sometimes the king forgot this. When King David broke the law and took another man's wife, the prophet Nathan told the king his sin and the king repented (2 Sam 12:7-13).

When King Ahab stole the property of an Israelite, the prophet Elijah confronted this king. Even this evil king humbled himself and repented (1 Kgs 21:17-29).

Despite his sins, King David was an ideal king. David was anointed king "to shepherd [God's] people Israel" (2 Sam 5:2). The shepherd motif is an important one in the Old Testament and in the Ancient Near East: a king like a shepherd should care for his people.

---

[1]Henri Berr, quoted by E. Jacob in *Theology of the Old Testament*, pp. 238-39.

It was said that King David "reigned over all Israel, doing what was just and right for all his people" (2 Sam 8:15). When David did what was wrong in respect to Uriah, he confessed his sin: "I have sinned against Yahweh" (2 Sam 12:13).

Justice and righteousness are the qualities of a good king. "The establishment and maintenance of justice [is the king's] primary obligation to Yahweh and the Israelite society."[2]

Psalm 72 is a prayer for the king. The prayer begins:

> Endow the king with your justice, O God, the royal son with your righteousness. May he judge your people in righteousness, your afflicted ones with justice.
>
> —Ps 72:1-2

A just king will care for the poor and needy. "May he defend the afflicted among the people and save the children of the needy; may he crush the oppressor" (Ps 72:4).

If a king rules with justice and righteousness, there will be shalom in the kingdom. Then "the mountains will bring shalom to the people." Then "the righteous will flourish; shalom will abound till the moon is no more" (Ps 72:3,7). Shalom is peace in a full, wholistic sense.

When there is no justice, there is no shalom. Jeremiah condemns King Jehoiakim:

> Woe to him who builds his palace by unrighteousness, his upper rooms by injustice, making his countrymen work for nothing, not paying them for their labor.
>
> -Sarcastically, Jeremiah asks,-
>
> Does it make you a king to have more and more cedar?
>
> —Jer 22:13,15

But Jehoiakim's father, King Josiah, was not like that.

---

[2]W. Brueggemann, *Theology of the Old Testament*, p. 611.

> Did not your father have food and drink? He did what was right
> and just, so all went with him. He defended the cause of the
> poor and needy, and so all went well.
>
> —Jer 22:15-16

God's words for Israel's rulers are relevant for our rulers today:

> Do what is just and right. Rescue from the hand of his
> oppressor the one who has been robbed. Do no wrong or
> violence to the alien, the fatherless or the widow, and do not
> shed innocent blood in this place.
>
> —Jer 22:3

Even the best kings or rulers make mistakes. Even King David sinned.
So the Old Testament anticipated a future king who would rule with
justice and righteousness.

Isaiah prophesied:

> A shoot will come up from the stump of Jesse; from his roots
> a Branch will bear fruit . . . with righteousness he will judge
> the needy, with justice he will give decisions for the poor of
> the earth.
>
> —Is 11:1,4

The rule of this Messiah would bring *shalom*:

> the wolf will live with the lamb, the leopard will lie down with
> the goat, the calf and the lion and the yearling together; and a
> little child will lead them.
>
> —Is 11:6

The messianic prophecies are a reminder to our society and to our
rulers of the ideals of justice and righteousness. When there is justice
and holiness, there is *shalom*.

Study Questions

1. How was Israel's society different from that of the nations around her?
2. According to Deuteronomy 17, how was the king to rule?
3. What does Psalm 72 tell us about the ideal king?
4. How is Jeremiah 22 relevant to our society today?
5. How is the messianic ideal relevant to our leaders today?

CHAPTER 15

PROPHETS IN ISRAEL

The priest was the regular spiritual leader of Israel. But in spiritual emergencies, God raised up prophets. The prophets were the Lord's fire brigade, raised up in special times to put out spiritual fires. While the office of priest was hereditary, the office of prophet was based on God's call.

The office of prophet developed in Israel's history. We should distinguish between early prophecy and later classical prophecy.

Early Prophecy

In their early days, prophets tended to live together in communities, something like monasteries today. These groups of prophets were centered at sanctuaries like Ramah, Gibeah, Bethel and Gilgal.[1] We see this in the stories of Samuel and Saul, and Elijah and Elisha.

When Samuel and Saul arrived in Gibeah, they were met by a band of prophets (1 Sam 10:10). In Ramah, Samuel was once leading a group of prophets who were prophesying (1 Sam 19:20). At the time of Elijah, Obadiah hid two groups of prophets in caves (1 Kgs 18:4). Later, Elijah and Elisha met companies of prophets in Bethel and Jericho (2 Kgs

---

[1] See E. Jacob, *Theology of the Old Testament*, pp. 239-40.

2:3,5). Elisha participated in the lives of companies of prophets after Elijah's departure (2 Kgs 4:38-41; 6:1-7).

Some of these prophets had unusual or ecstatic behavior. (The Greek word for "ecstatic" suggests one who is standing outside of his normal self.) When Elisha was asked for some military advice, he requested a harpist to play for him. Then, perhaps in a trance, Elisha heard God speak to him (2 Kgs 3:15-16).

Once the Spirit of God again came on King Saul, and he stripped off his clothes and prophesied; he lay that way all night (1 Sam 19:23-24).

Often the Spirit of God would cause prophets and others to prophesy. At Gibeah, Saul prophesied with the band of prophets (1 Sam 10:10). The same thing happened to the men who were sent to capture David at Ramah, including even King Saul himself (1 Sam 19:20-24).

Sometimes the early prophets were called seers, or those who see. These seers might see visions. They might also be soothsayers, able to see hidden things. When Saul's father's donkeys went missing, Saul and his servant went to Samuel, who was a man of God or a seer. The servant said that "everything he says comes true. . . . He will tell us what way to take" (1 Sam 9:6,8). The text says that in the past prophets were called seers (1 Sam 9:9).

Sometimes, though, these prophets with their unusual and ecstatic behavior had a bad reputation. In later years, a court official in Jerusalem commanded "any madman who acts like a prophet" to be put into prison (Jer. 29:26). The established monarchy and priesthood did not always know how to deal with these prophets.

Classical Prophecy

Classical prophecy generally refers to the "writing prophets" or the three major and twelve minor prophets. This prophecy began in the eighth century BC at the time of Hosea and Amos (ca 760-750 BC). But the ninth-century prophet Elijah (ca 850 BC) forms a transition from early prophetism to classical prophetism.

Classical prophets were individuals who received the word of God. It was the word of God that defines classical prophecy. Classical prophets tended not to be part of a group of prophets; they usually did not have ecstatic or unusual behavior; and they did not always see visions. It was the word of God that characterized their lives and their messages.

Classical prophets often criticized sinful society. A Jewish scholar said:

> The prophet is an iconoclast, challenging the apparently holy, revered, and awesome. . . . The words of the prophet are stern, sour, stinging. But behind his austerity is love and compassion. . . . The prophet is a watchman, a servant, a messenger of God. . . . [But] the prophet is more than a messenger. . . . He is a person who stands in the presence of God. . . . [He] discloses a divine pathos . . . The prophet hears God's voice and feels his heart.
> —A. Heschel, *The Prophets*, 1:10,12,20,21,24,26.

The word "prophesy" in Greek means to speak for God. The prophet is one who stands in the presence of God and receives God's word and speaks it to God's people. It is the word that characterizes the classical prophet.

A prophet is called by God. "It is certain that it is the call that he has received which characterizes the prophet."[2] A prophet is not a prophet because of birth; he is a prophet because God called him.

Amos said that he was not a prophet but a farmer. "But Yahweh took me from tending the flock and said to me, 'Go, prophesy to my people Israel'" (Amos 7:14-15). Isaiah had a vision of God who sent him (Is 6:1-8). Before Jeremiah was born, God appointed him as a prophet to the nations (Jer 1:5). Ezekiel was by the Kebar River in Babylon when God called him (Ezek 1-3).

The decisive quality of a prophet is that he speaks God's word. False prophets speak what they or their hearers want to hear. True prophets speak God's word.

The classic prophet is described in Deuteronomy 18. God will tell him what to speak: "I will put my words in his mouth, and he will tell them everything I command him" (Deut 18:18).

When Jeremiah was called, God touched his mouth and said, "Now I have put words into your mouth" (Jer 1:9). Jeremiah's job was to speak God's words.

God said to Ezekiel, "You must speak my words to them." He was then told to eat the scroll and was told, "Son of man, go now to the house of Israel and speak my words to them" (Ezek 2:7-3:4). The scroll was sweet, but the message was bitter.

The prophet Jeremiah distinguishes between the false prophets who claim they had a dream and the true prophet who speaks God's word: "Let the prophet who has a dream tell his dream, but let the one who has my word speak it faithfully" (Jer 23:28). Then God says that his word is "like fire and like a hammer that breaks a rock in pieces" (Jer 23:29). God's word spoken by a true prophet has power.

---

[2]E. Jacob, *Theology of the Old Testament*, p. 241.

The Message of the Prophets

The main message of the prophets is summed up in one Hebrew word: *shuv* (turn or return). "Return, faithless Israel . . . return, faithless people . . . return" (Jer 3:12,14,20).

The prophetic message presupposed the covenant made at Sinai. There Israel entered into a covenant agreement with God. The laws provided the conditions of this relationship. When Israel broke this relationship, the prophets called Israel to return to their covenant God.

But this covenant relationship was not just a legal contract. It was a personal relationship. God was the husband and Israel was the wife. God's wife had run off to be with another god. This made God sad. One commentator speaks of the sorrow and anguish in God's heart that resulted from Israel's prostitution.[3] God was like a wounded husband who pleads with his wife: "Return, faithless people, for I am your husband" (Jer. 3:14). There is *pathos* or passion in the heart of God.

The writings of the prophets consist mostly of oracles. An oracle is a divine utterance. In the text, an oracle is a passage (pericope) that is often set apart by messenger formulas like "thus says Yahweh" or "declares Yahweh."

There are three basic types of oracles in the prophets: oracles of judgment, oracles of exhortation, and oracles of salvation.[4] An exegete of the prophets should identify or "think oracles."[5]

The first two chapters of Amos have nine oracles of judgment. Most are set apart by the formulas "thus says Yahweh" and "declares Yahweh." Six of these oracles are words of judgment against the nations, but three are oracles of judgment against Judah and Israel. The purpose of these oracles against God's people is to cause them to repent.

---

[3] A. Heschel, *The Prophets*, 1:109-15.
[4] H.D. Preuss, *Old Testament Theology*, 2:76-81.
[5] G. Fee and D. Stuart, *How to Read the Bible for All Its Worth*, p. 158.

In the book of Amos, we also find oracles of exhortation. "Seek me and live" introduces an oracle of exhortation (Amos 5:4). Oracles of exhortation tell Israel what God expects of them.

The last five verses of Amos contain an oracle of salvation: "in that day I will restore David's fallen tent. . . . I will plant Israel in their own land" (Amos 9:11-15). Oracles of salvation are usually prophecies of hope about the future.

You can see that the majority of prophecy is not the prediction of the future (foretelling), but it is God's telling his people how to live (forth-telling). Only five verses of Amos are foretelling; the rest contains sermons calling Israel back to God. Prophecy then is not primarily the prediction of the future, but it is the speaking of God's word to his people in their present situation.

A true prophet is one who speaks the word of God. A false prophet speaks his own words. A preacher who brings God's word to his people faithfully is a true prophet. But to be a true prophet, one must read and listen carefully to God's Word. If we do not carefully exegete the Scriptures, then we may not be hearing or preaching God's word.

The Old Testament also anticipated the coming of an ideal prophet. Moses said, "Yahweh your God will raise up for you a prophet like me from among your own brothers. You must listen to him" (Deut 18:15). Jesus Christ is the Word of God (John 1:1). He was a prophet (as well as being a priest and king). Part of his ministry was to tell us who God is. He did this both by his life and his words.

Study Questions

1. Describe the differences between early prophetism and the classical prophets.
2. What is the definition of a prophet?
3. When did God raise up prophets?
4. What is the basic message of the prophets?
5. What are the three main types of prophetic oracles found in the Old Testament?
6. List and classify the nine prophetic oracles in Amos 1-2.
7. Why was God sad when Israel sinned?

CHAPTER 16

THE NATIONS AND GOD'S MISSION

The focus of the Old Testament seems to be on the people of Israel. Abraham and his descendants appear to be the main ethnic concern of the Hebrew Bible.

So is the Old Testament a particularistic book? What of the other tribes and nations? Is God interested in the peoples beyond Israel?

The Nations in God's Plan

The first chapters of Genesis are universal in their concern. Adam and Eve were the parents of the entire human race. But eventually "the earth was corrupt in God's sight and full of violence" (Gen 6:11). So God destroyed the earth with a flood and saved only Noah and his family.

Noah then was the father of the entire human race. The genealogy of Genesis 10 lists all the peoples of the earth. About 70 peoples or nations are listed. This genealogy is a statement that the nations are important in God's redemptive history.

The next chapter begins with a reference to "the whole earth" (Gen 11:1). The focus is still universal. But the whole world was going off the tracks. The people wanted to be equal to God. So God scattered them over the face of the whole earth. Then God chose Abram and his family.

The beginning of salvation history is thus universal in its scope. God worked with Adam and Eve, the parents of all mankind. God blessed Noah and his family, from whom all of mankind came.

But humanity rebelled against God at three significant moments. Adam and Eve disobeyed and were driven from the garden. The whole earth became corrupt and was destroyed by a flood. The whole world built a tower in pride and were scattered. It was only then that God chose Abraham and the people of Israel.

Israel as a Light to the Nations

The election of Abraham is described in Genesis 12. There God singles out Abraham and his family for special favor. God promises that his family would become a great nation and that he would be blessed (Gen 12:1-3).

The election of Abraham is a particularistic event. But the purpose of the election has a universal concern. The purpose of Abraham's election was so that "all peoples on earth [would] be blessed through [him]" (Gen 12:3). The election of a particular people was for the purpose that the entire world might receive God's blessing.

Genesis 1-11, then, is universal in scope. Genesis 12 through Malachi 4 is particularistic but with a universal concern. God wanted Abraham and his people to be a blessing to the nations.

After the exodus God made a covenant with Israel at Mount Sinai. God promised to enter into a special relationship with Israel. God told Israel that they were a "treasured possession" (Ex 19:5). But again the purpose of Israel's election was that the nations would be blessed. Israel was to be "a kingdom of priests and a holy nation" (Ex 19:6). All of Israel was to stand as a priest or a mediator between God and the nations. Israel was to show the nations what holiness is.

Of course Israel often failed in this assignment. But God's concern in the election of Abraham and Israel was that the nations would be blessed through Israel.

Later in Israel's history, God told Israel: "You are my witnesses and my servant whom I have chosen. . . . . You are my witnesses that I am God" (Is 43:10,12).

Centripetal Mission

In the New Testament, mission was centrifugal. Believers were sent out to proclaim the Gospel. "Go, and make disciples," Jesus said (Mt 28:19).

But in the Old Testament, mission tended to be centripetal. People were drawn in to Israel. They were attracted to Israel.

The Canaanite woman Rahab asked to be included in God's people when Jericho would be taken (Josh 2:9-13). The Moabite woman Ruth wanted Naomi's God to be her God (Ruth 1:16-17). The Syrian general Naaman learned that "there is no God in all the world except in Israel" (2 Kgs 5:15). The pagan sailors learned from a runaway prophet that Yahweh indeed is God, and then they sacrificed to Yahweh (Jon 1:16).

During the exile and dispersion of the Jewish people, there was a significant movement of Gentile people to the temple or synagogue. In a polytheistic world, the Jewish monotheism was attractive. In an immoral world, Israel's ethical standards were respected. Many proselytes and God-fearers attached themselves to the Jewish religion.

Mission in the Old Testament was largely centripetal. Gentiles were drawn into the sphere of Israel's faith.

Judgment on the Nations

Often in the Old Testament the nations were the objects of God's judgment. This is because the nations refused to believe in Yahweh and they worshiped false gods. Also, they usually did not conform to basic ethical standards found in creation.

Therefore, when Israel entered into the Promised Land they were commanded to destroy the nations there. "Make no treaty with them, and show them no mercy" (Deut 7:2). The book of Joshua describes the implementation of this policy.

This harsh policy was a reaction to the gross idolatry, immorality and social injustice in Canaan. It was also a precaution against possible syncretism. God said,

> You must not worship Yahweh your God in their way, because in worshiping their gods, they do all kinds of detestable things Yahweh hates.
>
> —Deut 12:31

Many of the prophetic books have oracles against the nations. (See Isaiah 13-23, Jeremiah 46-51, Ezekiel 25-32, Amos 1-2 and Zephaniah 2.) There the nations around Israel were judged because of their idolatry and wickedness. These oracles assert "that the nations are subject to a governance, a requirement, and an expectation." Under God's sovereignty, "there is a kind of international law or code of human standards . . . that requires every nation to act in civility and humaneness toward others."[1] Refusal to live up to God's natural law has negative consequences.

Three superpowers stand out for God's judgment: Egypt, Assyria and Babylon.[2] Egypt, who enslaved Israel, was an oppressor. The

---

[1] W. Brueggemann, *Theology of the Old Testament*, p. 503.
[2] W. Brueggemann, *Theology of the Old Testament*, pp. 504-15.

armies of Assyria and Babylon were ruthless. All three of these superpowers displayed enormous arrogance. So God promised that these superpowers would fall and God's chosen people would be preserved.

The Nations Will Praise God

Often the Old Testament has a negative view of the nations. But there is a surprising expectation that the nations will praise God.

The psalms often call on the nations to praise God. "Praise Yahweh, all you nations; extol him, all you peoples" (Ps 117:1). "Ascribe to Yahweh, O families of nations, ascribe to Yahweh glory and strength" (Ps 96:7).

Psalm 67 contains a prayer that the peoples and nations might praise God: "May the peoples praise you, O God; may all the peoples praise you" (Ps 67:3). Psalm 86 contains the expectation that this will happen: "All the nations you have made will come and worship before you, O Yahweh" (Ps 86:9).

The prophets also had an expectation that the nations would worship God. Isaiah predicts:

> In the last days the mountain of Yahweh's temple will be established as chief among the mountains . . . and all nations will stream to it.
>
> —Is 2:2

This prophecy was fulfilled with the first coming of Jesus.

The Old Testament may appear to be particularistic. But the election of Abraham and Israel has a universal purpose. God's intention and salvation plan is that all nations praise God.

Study Questions

1. Describe the universalistic focus of Genesis 1-11.
2. Describe the purpose of the election of Abraham and Israel.
3. Describe the missiological message of Psalm 67.
4. Give examples of centrifugal and centripetal mission.
5. Describe the fulfillment of Isaiah 2:2-5.

CHAPTER 17

THE FUTURE

Although most of the prophetic message speaks to Israel's contemporary situation, there are expectations of God's future acting in history. These expectations center on the coming day of Yahweh and the messianic kingdom.

The Day of Yahweh

There was a popular belief in Israel during the time of Amos that God would come to destroy the pagan nations and to save Israel (see Amos 5:18). The Old Testament prophets shared this concept of the day of the Lord, but they redefined it.

The day of Yahweh (*yom Yahweh*) is a day when God would come in power to judge the wicked and to save the righteous. The focus of this concept is the *coming* of Yahweh.

When a holy God comes to visit the earth, then something will happen. There will be judgment for those who oppose this God, and there will be salvation for those who are faithful.

One theologian tells us that the language of the day of Yahweh in the Old Testament is the language of holy war. When God comes, he will defeat his enemies. There will be disaster for the enemy. It will be a great day.[1]

However, God will not just come once. Before the final day of Yahweh, there are other times when God comes in power. For Joel, the plague of locusts was a day of Yahweh (Joel 2:1-11). "The overthrow of Jerusalem was a day of Yahweh."[2] Isaiah (22:5-13) and Zephaniah (1:4-13) prophesied this day. The destruction of Babylon was also a day of Yahweh. God came in power and destroyed this superpower (Is 13:6-9).

The surprise for the people in Amos' day was that the day of Yahweh would not necessarily be good news for Israel. The Israelites assumed that since they were God's elect and covenant people, God would be on their side. But Amos' unique message was that God is against the wicked, whether they be from the nations or from Israel. The day of Yahweh would be darkness for Israel, not light; it would be judgment, not salvation (Amos 5:18-20).

In addition to these intermediate days of Yahweh, there would be a great, final day of the Lord. Joel speaks of signs and wonders in the heavens "before the coming of the great and dreadful day of Yahweh" (Joel 2:30-31). Obadiah says that "the day of Yahweh is near for all nations" (Obad 1:15). The last chapter of Zechariah portrays the day of Yahweh as a final battle (Zech 14).

The prophecy of a future day of Yahweh is a warning to every person. Those who are wicked will be judged. But "everyone who calls on the name of Yahweh will be saved" (Joel 2:32).

---

[1] G. von Rad, *Theology of the Old Testament*, 2:119-25.

[2] G. von Rad, "Hemera," in *Theological Dictionary of the New Testament*, 2:944.

The Messiah

The Old Testament also had an expectation of a future king in the line of David who would rule over his people. This king was the promised Messiah.

The Hebrew word *mashiah* or Messiah means the anointed one. (A Greek translation of *mashiah* is *christos* or Christ.) The word *mashiah* in the Old Testament usually refers to the anointed king. King Saul is often called Yahweh's anointed (e.g., 1 Sam 26:9,11,16,23). David is also Yahweh's anointed (e.g., 1 Sam 16:6). The Davidic king is also God's anointed (e.g., Pss 18:50; 20:6).

The word Messiah was used in the intertestamental period to refer to the coming Davidic king. The Jews in the New Testament were expecting the promised Messiah.

The basis of the messianic expectation was the prophecy of Nathan to King David. Then Nathan said to David, "Your house and your kingdom will endure forever before me; your throne will be established forever" (2 Sam 7:16).

The prophets after David began to expect this Davidic king. A few decades before the end of the northern kingdom, the prophet Amos said, "In that day I will restore David's fallen tent" (Amos 9:11). A messianic king would come to occupy the throne of David.

Micah expected a ruler to proceed from the town of Bethlehem (Mic 5:2). Micah's contemporary, the prophet Isaiah, expected a royal son who would "reign on David's throne . . . with justice and righteousness" (Is 9:6-7). Isaiah also expected a shoot from Jesse's stump who would judge the needy with justice and righteousness (Is 11:1-5).

The prophet Jeremiah expected a Davidic king who would reign with justice and righteousness (Jer 23:5-6; 33:15-16). Ezekiel also prophesied a Davidic king who would shepherd God's people (Ezek 34:23-24; 37:24-25).

Other prophecies in the Old Testament also point to a future Messiah. All of these prophecies are fulfilled in Jesus Christ. The angel Gabriel told Mary that Jesus would reign on the throne of David forever (Lk 1:32-33). At Caesarea Philippi, Peter correctly identified Jesus as being the *christos* or the Messiah (Mk 8:29).

The Messianic Kingdom

A true king will have a kingdom. The Old Testament prophets describe this kingdom. We should remember that prophetic language is often symbolic. It would be wrong to take these prophecies too literally. So what will this messianic kingdom be like?

The prophets tell us that the Messiah, the son of David, would be the king. He would rule with justice and righteousness. We have seen that Isaiah and Jeremiah prophesied that the Messiah would rule with justice (Is 11:4; Jer 23:5). Ezekiel pictures the Messiah as being a shepherd for the people (Ezek 34:23; 37:24).

The reign of the messianic King would be characterized by peace and prosperity. Amos speaks of bountiful harvests (Amos 9:13-15). Micah and Isaiah speak of peace between the nations when the people would turn swords into plowshares (Mic 4:3; Is 2:4). Isaiah offers an idyllic picture of violent animals living together with peaceful ones (Is 11:6-9). Ezekiel talks of a covenant of peace when danger will be removed and peace and prosperity will prevail (Ezek 34:25-29).

In the messianic kingdom, God's word would be preached. "The law will go out from Zion, the word of Yahweh from Jerusalem" (Mic 4:2; Is 2:3).

In the messianic kingdom, the hearts of God's people would be changed. God said,

> I will give you a new heart and put a new spirit in you; I will
> remove from you your heart of stone and give you a heart of
> flesh.
>
> —Ezek 36:26

In the messianic kingdom, God's people would be in a renewed relation
with God. Ezekiel uses the old covenant formula: "You will be my
people, and I will be your God" (Ezek 36:28), and "I will be their God,
and they will be my people" (Ezek 37:27).

This is what Jeremiah calls the new covenant. Yahweh said,

> The time is coming when I will make a new covenant with the
> house of Israel . . . . I will put my law in their minds and write it
> on their hearts. I will be their God, and they will be my people.
>
> —Jer 31:31-33

The Holy Spirit would be part of the messianic kingdom. He is the one
who would soften the hearts of God's people. The prophet Joel said
that "afterward . . . before the coming of the great and dreadful day of
Yahweh," God would pour out his Spirit on all people (Joel 2:28-31).

So when is this messianic Kingdom? When is this time of
peace and prosperity? When will the Messiah reign with justice and
righteousness? When is this eschatological kingdom of God?

The kingdom of God is a future, eschatological concept. When we
die and if we believe, we will enter the future kingdom of God. Then
there will be no more tears and no more suffering.

But when Jesus began his ministry, he said that this eschatological
kingdom is nearby or "at hand" (Mk 1:15; Mt. 4:17). When John the
Baptist asked if the messianic kingdom was here, Jesus told him that
already the blind see, the deaf hear, the dead are raised, and the good
news is being preached to the poor (Matt 11:4-5). The kingdom of God
was already present at Jesus' first coming!

The apostle Paul said that this present kingdom of God is "righteousness, peace and joy in the Holy Spirit" (Rom. 14:17). The pictures of righteousness and peace in Isaiah and Micah have their fulfillment in the kingdom of God, which is both present and future.

In this kingdom of God, Jesus is already ruling. When Jesus ascended into heaven, he sat at the right hand of God and was given all authority (Eph 1:20-23). Jesus is reigning now! "He must reign until he has put all his enemies under his feet" (1 Cor 15:25).

The Old Testament prophets prophesied this messianic kingdom that was fulfilled in Jesus. If we believe in the Messiah, we can enjoy this peace and prosperity right now. If we believe in the Messiah, we have the fruits of the Spirit now. But in the future kingdom we will enjoy perfect peace and righteousness and prosperity.

Study Questions

1. What is the day of the Lord?
2. What does the Hebrew word "Messiah" mean? What is the Greek translation of "Messiah"?
3. Describe the messianic kingdom as prophesied in the Old Testament.
4. Describe the messianic kingdom in Matthew 13.
5. Is the kingdom of God present or future? Explain.

CHAPTER 18

EXCURSUS

The Discipline of Old Testament Theology

Old Testament theology is a part of biblical theology. In the early, medieval and Reformation church there was no biblical theology or Old Testament theology as such. There was just general theology.

Tertullian, Augustine and Martin Luther did not do biblical theology by itself. Instead, they did general Christian theology.

The origins of biblical theology as a separate discipline go back to Germany in the eighteenth century. On March 30, 1787, Johann Gabler delivered a famous lecture calling for the separation of biblical theology from dogmatic or systematic theology.

Biblical theology was to look at the historical dimension of Scripture. What was the historical background to each book of the Bible? What is the unique message of the individual books or parts of Scripture?

Systematic theology, on the other hand, focused on questions of belief. What do we believe in our respective church traditions or as Christians?

This distinction was to a certain extent useful. Why, for example, is the history of David in the book of Kings different from the same history in Chronicles? Old Testament theology can help us understand the difference between the two books.

(The book of Kings was completed during the exile when Israel had broken the covenant; the book of Chronicles was written after the exile when the Jews were a small and discouraged people back in Jerusalem. So the book of Kings tells of some of the mistakes of David to teach us a lesson; but the book of Chronicles portrays the good side of David to encourage a tiny remnant.)

But soon Old Testament theology was reduced to historical questions. Matters of faith were excluded. "The historical approach had triumphed on every side." The result was "the tyranny of historicism in OT studies."[1]

The matter was complicated with the advent of Julius Wellhausen. In 1878 he published his *Prolegomena to the History of Ancient Israel*. In this book he laid the foundations of the documentary hypothesis. He thought that there were four basic sources for the Pentateuch and other parts of Scripture: a Jahwist, an Elohist, the Deuteronomist and the priestly sources. (This is the "JEDP" theory.)

This radical cutting up of Scripture was highly speculative. It must be emphasized that the documentary hypothesis is an unproven theory, just like Darwin's theory of evolution, which was developed at the same time.

You will discover that many books in a standard theological library have documentary presuppositions. A critical student should not accept everything that is written in a book. A critical student will evaluate the presuppositions of every book that he or she reads.

By 1900 Old Testament theology was almost dead. Old Testament theology had been reduced to historical questions. But in the twentieth century Old Testament theology was revived in Germany.

---

[1]W. Eichrodt, *Old Testament Theology* 1:29,31.

In the 1930s Walter Eichrodt published his *Theology of the Old Testament.* He used the historical-systematic method to understand the main themes of the Old Testament. Eichrodt's theology is synchronic (systematic) built around the theme of the covenant.

In 1957 and 1960, Gerhard von Rad published his two-volume *Old Testament Theology.* His theology is diachronic, tracing Israel's confessions of God's salvation history through time. ("Diachronic" means "through time"; "synchronic" means "at the same time.")

Eichrodt and von Rad revived Old Testament theology. We are grateful to them for this. But one must again evaluate their presuppositions. Both of them accept the unproven, evolutionary documentary hypothesis. Also, von Rad in particular questions the historicity of many of the events in the Old Testament. He even questions the historical nature of Moses and the exodus.

As evangelicals, we hold to the authority of the Old and New Testaments as the Word of God. We also believe that the historical events in Scripture actually happened. If we make use of scholarly works, we have to examine their presuppositions.

Some Old Testament commentaries spend much of their time looking at the theology of the alleged J or E or D or P sources, but in the end they miss the theology of the Holy Spirit in the canon itself.

So in 1970 Brevard Childs blew the whistle. Everyone was off sides! In his *Biblical Theology in Crisis* and subsequent publications, Childs posited the canonical approach to biblical theology. The canon of Scripture in its final form is the Word of God that should be the source of our theology. We should not worry excessively about hypothetical sources; instead we should be listening to the canon itself.

Old Testament theology since this time has been diverse. There has been a large variety of significant studies since 1970. Evangelical scholars have also made important contributions.

But the last few decades have seen the rise of postmodernism. Postmodernism is the belief that there is no absolute truth. A Scripture text can have many different meanings. This is in contrast to the traditional view that a text has one meaning but many applications.

(If a student writes a letter asking for school fees or proposing marriage to a young lady, the letter will have only one meaning. However someone can use that letter to make personal applications to his own situation. In the same way, a Scripture text has only one original meaning but many possible applications to people in different situations. It is wrong to say that a single Bible text has many meanings.)

Walter Brueggemann is a postmodernist. He thinks that there is no one correct interpretation of a text. A text, he thinks, has many different meanings.[2] But the tragic result of this process is that the Old Testament is no longer the Word of God; instead the text, he thinks, can be used by different people in different contexts to say different things. Scripture then loses its authority in our lives.

Brueggemann, however, takes the text of Scripture very seriously. Evangelicals too take the text of Scripture seriously. So one can use Brueggemann because of his deep understanding of the Old Testament text, but one should always be aware of his postmodern presuppositions.

Justin Ukpong also shares these postmodernist presuppositions. He thinks that "the meaning of a text is a function of the interaction between the text in its context and the reader in his/her context." Thus, "there is no one absolute meaning of a text to be recovered through historical analysis alone."[3]

---

[2]W. Brueggemann, *Theology of the Old Testament*, pp. 61-66.

[3]Justin Ukpong, "Developments in Biblical Interpretation in Africa: Historical and Hermeneutical Directions," in *The Bible in Africa*, p. 24.

However, as evangelicals we believe that the Old Testament is the authoritative Word of God. We believe that the grammatico-historical method of exegesis is a proper method to discover the original meaning of a text. There is an absolute meaning of a text which exegetical and hermeneutical methods strive to discover.

The Old Testament is the Word of God. We should listen carefully to this Word. This Word should shape and form our theology.

As evangelicals we also believe that the Old Testament points to Jesus Christ. In the end, all of Scripture proclaims Jesus Christ. The Old Testament anticipates the Messiah; the New Testament fully describes who Jesus is. Both the Old and New Testaments proclaim God's salvation history that finds its fulfillment in the person of Jesus Christ.

BIBLIOGRAPHY

Anderson, Bernhard. *Contours of Old Testament Theology*. Minneapolis: Fortress, 1999.

Baab, Otto. *The Theology of the Old Testament*. Nashville: Abingdon, 1949.

Barth, C. *God with Us*. Grand Rapids: Eerdmans, 1991.

Blenkinsopp, Joseph. *Sage, Priest, Prophet*. Louisville: Westminster John Knox Press, 1995.

Blenkinsopp, Joseph. *Wisdom and Law in the Old Testament*. Oxford: Oxford University Press, 1995.

Brueggemann, Walter. *Theology of the Old Testament*. Minneapolis: Fortress, 1997.

Childs, Brevard. *Biblical Theology in Crisis*. Philadelphia: Westminster, 1970.

Childs, Brevard. *Old Testament Theology in a Canonical Context*. Philadelphia: Fortress, 1985.

Clements, R.E. *Old Testament Theology*. Atlanta: John Knox, 1978.

Clements, R.E. *Wisdom in Theology*. Grand Rapids: Eerdmans, 1992.

Crenshaw, James. *Old Testament Wisdom*. Louisville: Westminster John Knox, 1998.

Davidson, A.B. *The Theology of the Old Testament*. New York: Scribners, 1904.

De Vries, S.J. "Sin, Sinner" in *Interpreter's Dictionary of the Bible* 4:361-376. Nashville: Abingdon, 1962.

Dyrness, William. *Themes in Old Testament Theology*. Downers Grove: InterVarsity, 1977.

Eichrodt, Walther. *Theology of the Old Testament*. 2 vols. Trans. J. Baker. Philadelphia: Westminster, 1961, 1967.

Fee, Gordon and Douglas Stuart. *How to Read the Bible for All Its Worth*. Grand Rapids: Zondervan, 1982; Jos: Potters House, 1999.

Fretheim, Terence. *God and World in the Old Testament*. Nashville: Abingdon, 2005.

Gammie, John. *Holiness in Israel*. Minneapolis: Fortress, 1989.

Goldingay, John. *Old Testament Theology*. 3 vols. Downers Grove: InterVarsity, 2003, 2006, 2009.

Herbert, A.S. *Worship in Ancient Israel*. London: Lutterworth, 1959.

Heschel, Abraham. *The Prophets*. 2 vols. London: Lutterworth, 1962.

Hoekema, Anthony. *Created in God's Image*. Grand Rapids: Eerdmans, 1986.

House, Paul. *Old Testament Theology*. Downers Grove: InterVarsity, 1998.

Jacob, Edmond. *Theology of the Old Testament*. Trans. A. Heathcote and P. Allcock. New York: Harper, 1958.

Kaiser, Walter. *Toward an Old Testament Theology*. Grand Rapids: Zondervan, 1978.

Knight, G.A.C. *A Christian Theology of the Old Testament*. Richmond: John Knox, 1959, 1964.

Martens, E.A. *God's Design*. Grand Rapids: Baker, 1981, 1994.

Mendenhall, G.E. "Covenant" in *Interpreter's Dictionary of the Bible*, I: 714-23. Nashville: Abingdon, 1962.

Merrill, Eugene. *Everlasting Dominion: A Theology of the Old Testament*. Nashville: Broadman and Holman, 2006.

Murphy, Roland. *The Tree of Life*. Grand Rapids: Eerdmans, 1996.

NIV Study Bible. Ed. K. Barker et al. Grand Rapids: Zondervan, 1985.

Payne, J.B. *The Theology of the Older Testament*. Grand Rapids: Zondervan, 1962.

Preuss, Horst D. *Old Testament Theology*. 2 vols. Trans. L. Perdue. Louisville: Westminster John Knox, 1995, 1996.

Ringren, H. "Tame," in *Theological Dictionary of the Old Testament,* 5:330-32. Grand Rapids: Eerdmans, 1986.

Rodd, Cyril. *Glimpses of a Strange Land.* Edinburgh: T & T Clark, 2001.

Routledge, Robin. *Old Testament Theology: A Thematic Approach.* Nottingham: Apollos, 2008.

Rowley, H.H. *Worship in Ancient Israel: Its Forms and Meaning.* Philadelphia: Fortress, 1967.

Smith, Ralph. *Old Testament Theology.* Nashville: Broadman, 1993.

Ukpong, Justin. Justin. "Developments in Biblical Interpretation in Africa: Historical and Hermeneutical Directions", in *The Bible in Africa,* pp. 11-28. Edited by G. West and M. Dube. Leiden: Brill, 2000.

von Rad, Gerhard. "Hemera," in *Theological Dictionary of the New Testament,* 2:943-47. Grand Rapids: Eerdmans, 1964.

von Rad, Gerhard. *Old Testament Theology.* 2 vols. Translated by D. Stalker. London: Oliver and Boyd, 1962, 1965.

Vriezen, T. C. *An Outline of Old Testament Theology.* Translated by S. Neuijen. Oxford: Blackwell, 1958, 1970.

Waltke, Bruce. *An Old Testament Theology.* Grand Rapids: Zondervan, 2007.

Wolff, H.W. *Anthropology of the Old Testament.* Translated by M. Kohl. London: SCM Press, 1974.

Wright, Christopher. *Living as the People of God.* Leicester: InterVarsity, 1983.

Zimmerli, W. *Old Testament Theology in Outline.* Translated by D. Green. Atlanta: John Knox, 1978.

9 789789 051175